SIX THEOSOPHIC POINTS

AND OTHER WRITINGS

SIX THEOSOPHIC POINTS

AND OTHER WRITINGS

BY

JACOB BOEHME

With an Introductory Essay
UNGROUND AND FREEDOM
BY NICOLAS BERDYAEV

Ann Arbor Paperbacks
THE UNIVERSITY OF MICHIGAN PRESS

Third printing 1971
First edition as an Ann Arbor Paperback 1958
All rights reserved
ISBN 0-472-06017-1
Translated by John Rolleston Earle
The translation of the introductory essay
Unground and Freedom, prepared at the University of Michigan, is
copyright © by the University of Michigan 1958
Published in the United States of America by
The University of Michigan Press and simultaneously
in Don Mills, Canada, by Longman Canada Limited
Manufactured in the United States of America

UNGROUND AND FREEDOM
by Nicolas Berdyaev

I

Jacob Boehme, beyond a doubt, is one of the greatest of Christian gnostics. I am using the word not in the sense of the heresies of the opening centuries of the Christian era, but to indicate a wisdom grounded in revelation and employing myths and symbols rather than concepts—a wisdom much more contemplative than discursive. Such is religious philosophy, or theosophy.

Nothing is more characteristic of Boehme than his great simplicity of heart and childlike purity of soul. These alone explain how he could call out at the moment of death: "And now, I'll take the road to Paradise." He was not a scholar nor a lettered man nor a schoolman, but simply a craftsman shoemaker. He was of the class of wise men that come from the people. He knew no more of Aristotle than of the pseudo-Dionysius the Areopagite, medieval Scholasticism, or medieval mysticism. There are in him no direct influences of Neoplatonism, as there are in the majority of Christian mystics. The Bible was his principal spiritual sustenance, though he also read Paracelsus, Sebastian Frank, Weigel, Schwenkfeld. He lived within the mystic-theosophic currents of the Germany of his time. He was never a philosopher in the school sense of the word; above all else he was a visionary theosopher and a creator of myths, and yet his influence on German philosophy is enormous. He thought not in clear-cut concepts but through symbols and myths. It was his conviction that Christianity was being distorted by scholars, theologians, popes, and cardinals. He was himself of the Lutheran confession, and a minister escorted him to his last resting place. But the Lutheran clergy persecuted him, hounded him, forbade the printing of his writings. This is typical of all creeds; but he, as most mystics and theosophists, was above creeds.

Strong Catholic elements can be discerned in Boehme's work, in spite of his hatred of papism. To state precisely the sources of his wisdom is a highly complex problem, the problem of the possibility of a personal, gnostic revelation and illumination, of a supernatural charismatic gift. Although today we are led to believe far more strongly than we used to that Boehme was a reader, it is nonetheless certain that his doctrine cannot be explained by influences or by borrowings (one could not say as much for any other original and at all profound thinker). Eckhardt was a man of scholarship and letters; he knew Aristotle, the pseudo-Dionysius, St. Thomas Aquinas, as well as medieval Scholasticism and mysticism. Boehme, beyond a doubt, had original intuitions.

He himself speaks of the sources of his wisdom: "I can do nothing with their methods and their formulas, since I have not studied by them. I have another master, and that is all Nature. In Nature and its creative force I have studied and learned my philosophy, my astrology, and my theology—not through the mediation of men." One senses here the revolt of the Renaissance against Scholasticism.

At the same time Boehme is convinced that he arrives at his knowledge not by his own human powers, but through the intercession of the Holy Spirit. "By my own powers I am as blind as the next man and can do nothing, but through the Spirit of God, my own inborn spirit pierces all things—though not always with enough perseverance. When the Spirit of Divine Love passes through my spirit then the animal creature and the divinity form but one single being, one single conception, and one single light!"

Sophia herself helps him to pierce the divine mysteries. He believes that God "will adopt you like a beloved child, and make you put on the habit of the noble virgin Sophia and slip on the finger of your heart the ring of the Great Mystery, and only in this habit (of the new birth) will you have the power to speak of the eternal birth of God."

In contrast to most mystics, Boehme speaks of what pertains to God, the world, and man, and not of what happens to himself; he does not write a word about his own soul, nor about his spiritual way. This trait is precisely what sets theosophic mysticism apart from mysticism generally. The mystic of Boehme is of the gnostic type. But he arrives at the knowledge of God and of the world through man, his knowledge emanates from the subject and not from the object, in spite of the preponderant role he accords to the philosophy of nature and to cosmology. The visible world is the image of the invisible world. "The visible world is a manifestation of the interior spiritual world of eternal Light and Darkness, of that spiritual activity; it is a reflection of eternity which allows eternity to make itself visible." Heaven springs open within man. "Nor have I ascended into heaven, nor have I seen all the works and creations of God, but heaven has revealed itself within my spirit in such a way that I there recognize the divine works and creations." To Boehme, the physical, natural elements are at the same time of the psychic order. He sees in nature the same thing that he sees in the spirit. Man is a "microtheos and a microcosmos." The human soul contains both heaven and hell. Only in this way can God and the world be known. The spiritual and invisible world is the foundation of the material and visible world. God can be found only in the depths of one's own heart. It is vain to seek divine wisdom in academies and books.

Boehme's concept of the world is entirely symbolic. The whole of the visible world is symbol of the interior world. "The whole world, exterior and visible, with its essence, is but a sign or an appearance of the world that is interior and spiritual; everything that is interior and latent has an exterior correspondent." Physical qualities represent spiritual qualities. The foreword of Boehme's major work *Mysterium Magnum* starts with the affirmation that the visible world is the "symbol of the spiritual invisible world." Visible and sensible things are a form of being of the invisible; from the inapparent and the inconceivable are born the apparent and the conceivable. The world is symbol of God. "This world is an image of the divine essence and is God revealed through an earthly image." To know God means to see him being born in one's own soul. Such knowledge is possible only through the purification of the soul by the grace of the spirit of God. Boehme sees clearly the limits of human knowledge, and speaks of the stupidity of human wisdom. Yet he holds at the same time the highest view of knowledge itself. To know God is a duty of man—man was created for it. Boehme is a symbolist but not an idealist in the sense of the German idealism of the nineteenth century. He is a realist. He has not lost the living touch with real existence; he has not locked himself in the world of abstract thought, apart from being, nor in the world of subjective personal experiences.

For Boehme, knowledge has a realistic and symbolic character. To know the spiritual world meant for him to immerse oneself in this world. Existence has not for him become transformed in an object opposed to the subject. Knowledge is realized in existence itself; it is an event that takes place within being. The gnosis of Boehme was entirely of experience and of life, born of torments about the fate of man and of the world. His soul was a soul pure and good and full of compassion. But his feeling for the life of the world was hard and far from sentimental. His fundamental intuition about the existence of the world was an intuition of fire. This makes him kindred to Heraclitus. He had a particularly sharp and strong feeling for the evil in the life of the world. He sees everywhere a pitched battle between contrary principles, between light and darkness. In this feeling for the power of evil and the battle between God and the devil, light and darkness, he is close to the sources of the Reformation and the experience of Luther. He perceives

God not only as love but also as wrath. He is sensitive to what is bitter and sharp in God. Here physical qualities signify spiritual qualities. Within divinity itself he sees the dark nature which is an irrational abyss. In his view of life, Boehme stands at the threshold of the modern age. His roots are sunk deep into the Middle Ages, for he has not shaken off medieval mystic realism. But already there rises in him the blood of a man of the Reformation and of the Renaissance. He shows an altogether "renaissance" attitude toward the life of the cosmos and toward nature, and a consciousness of himself far above that of a man of the Middle Ages. In the dynamism of his concept of the world, in the interest he shows in origin and becoming, in his feeling for the battle of opposing elements and for the idea of freedom—which, to him, is primary—Boehme is a man of the modern age. He no longer conceives of the world as an eternally static order nor as a hierarchical and unmoving system. The life of the world is a battle, a becoming, a vast process, all fire and dynamism. There is no resemblance here to the world view of Aquinas or of Dante.

Boehme has thought more deeply than the men of the Middle Ages upon the problem of the origin of evil, the problem of theodicy. How God could create the world, foreseeing evil and suffering—that was a question which tormented him greatly. He sought salvation in the heart of the Son Jesus, because he found in the Father nothing but wrath and in the world nothing but evil and suffering. There was a moment when Boehme believed that God had quitted this evil world, and he then searched for a nearer God. As Koyré very rightly observed, Boehme started from

the torments about the problem of evil and sought
salvation first of all, and only then knowledge. How
to understand evil, in the face of the absoluteness of
divinity? How to escape the divine wrath of a God
who had not yet revealed himself in the Son, as love?
Boehme's torment over the problem of evil relates
him to the ancient gnostics. But his conclusions differ
from theirs, by his incomparably more Christian character. At any rate, Boehme belonged in that category
of people who have been grievously hurt by the evil
and tortures of life in the world. The first in the history of modern thought, Boehme made a discovery
that was to be of immense importance to German
idealism—that a thing can be revealed only through
another thing that resists it. Light cannot reveal itself without darkness, nor good without evil, nor the
spirit without the resistance of matter.

II

Boehme wants to resolve a question that has troubled many a philosopher: How is the transition (or
passage) from God to the world possible?—from the
one to the many, from the eternal to the temporal?
How has Divine Trinity come into being? How was
the creation of the world possible out of a divine
nothing, an absolute? In what manner did the Creator
appear? How did Personality disclose itself in God?
The absolute of apophatic theology and of metaphysics cannot be Creator of the world. This God,
Creator of cataphatic theology, is correlative to creation, to man. It had been the same even with Meister
Eckhardt.

I do not mean to develop here Boehme's doctrine

on the Trinity. His formulations in this order of
thought are not always distinguished by precision, and
do not satisfy the dogmatic. But what impresses me
is that everywhere in the universe and in man Boehme
sees a threefold principle, image of the Divine Trinity.
Orthodox theology has always been troubled by the
fact that Boehme taught a theogonic process in God,
that he spoke of divine birth and of movement in God.
His concept of God was dynamic to the highest degree. The Christian theological systems have elabor-
ated a doctrine of God within the categories of Greek
philosophical thought. Thus, the doctrine of God as
pure act, containing within himself nothing that is
potential, is based entirely on Aristotle. Christian
theology has drawn its teaching of an immobile, satisfied, and static God not from the Bible, nor from
Christian revelation, but rather from Parmenides,
Plato, and Aristotle. The static nature of Greek ontology has left its imprint upon Christian theology.
The immobile God, God as pure act, is a concept of
God, it is not a living God. The predominant theological doctrine takes from God all inner life, denies
all process within him, likens Him to a motionless
rock. That idea is idolatrous. The God of the Bible
and of the Apocalypse is not so. He is full of a dra-
matic inner life. He has movement within Him.

The God who suffers the pain of the cross and the
passions, offering the sacrifice of love, is a moving
and not an unmoving God. Even St. Augustine recognized a certain movement in God. Louis de Blois de-
fined God as a solitary, un-understood martyr, and
was more convincing than St. Thomas Aquinas.
Boehme's immense importance lies in the fact that he

introduced into the concept of God a dynamic principle opposed to the static concept of Greek philosophy and medieval Scholasticism—in other words, he saw in God an internal life, a tragic nature that belongs to all life. This view Boehme owed to the fact that he had, on the one hand, made the Bible his spiritual nourishment and meditated upon it free from the categories of Greek gods; and on the other hand, he had introduced into his contemplation of God the experience of evil in the life of the world: the opposing forces tearing at it, the battle between light and darkness, sweet and bitter, love and anger. Boehme was a new soul, who took his stand face to face with the problem of evil, but who could no longer bow humbly and be satisfied with the knowledge of being a sinner. Daring, he wanted to know the origin and the meaning of evil. To this extent he was a gnostic. He saw a dark principle in all the primary sources of existence, more deeply than he saw existence itself. He was compelled to admit such a principle in Deity itself, and even a positive sense in the very existence of the evil that troubled him so much.

But he did not fall into the dualistic error of the Manichean gnostics, the error of a double divinity. Good cannot be conceived without evil. Good reveals itself through evil. By the nature of his reasoning on things divine, Boehme is not a Neoplatonic as were most of the Christian mystics. Nor is he a monist, nor does he teach emanation. For him, there is everywhere only will and opposition. In Boehme, Luther's feeling of evil becomes a metaphysical feeling. His metaphysics is voluntaristic, not intellectual as was that of Greece and the Middle Ages. Boehme's voluntarism is a new principle, which will be developed later in German philosophy. Boehme's philosophy of freedom was possible only thanks to this voluntarism. He is entirely imbued with a magic will which at its foundation is still dark and irrational. He faces the problem of evil with a deep earnestness that does not flinch before any consequence, and not as an educator or moralist using it to educate the young. For Boehme, existence is a stream of fire. This fire in the darkness is cold and searing. "All life is fire." The fire is will. A debased and famished will constitutes the first foundation of existence. Light and love come to its encounter. Darkness is virtually contained in the depth of existence, even within the Deity.

Darkness is tied up with meontic freedom. Boehme's doctrine of the Unground, the dark and irrational abyss that precedes being—a doctrine full of mystery—is an attempt to answer the question, basic before all others, of the appearance of the world and evil. Boehme's entire doctrine on the Unground is so closely intertwined with this doctrine of freedom that it is impossible to separate the two. I myself am inclined to interpret the Unground as an absolutely original freedom, something that is not even the meontic freedom determined by God. We shall see that Boehme's doctrine of the Unground lacks the sharpness that behooves a concept. Nor can we demand that sharpness since such a concept of the Unground is hardly possible—here is a realm beyond the limits of rational concepts. What, then, is the position of Boehme's doctrine in respect of traditional, rational theology which recognizes nothing that would correspond to the Unground?

I myself have always thought that the theodicy built up by the ruling systems of rational theology turns the relation between God and the world into a comedy, a game that God plays with himself and that reflects man's ancient enslavement, dejection, and fear. This is the ontology of sin. Boehme, on the other hand, wants to understand the mystery of the creation of the universe as a tragedy not merely human but divine as well. The only thing that saves rational cataphatic theology is the fact that there comes a moment when it changes into apophatic theology and asserts that we are face to face with a mystery both inconceivable and inexpressible, to which we must bow. But cataphatic theology takes the turn toward mystery, the only salvation and the only issue, much too late—and only after rationalizing everything in an unbearable manner. Theology goes too straight and too far in the rationalization of the divine mysteries, and is too hasty in pronouncing its veto against knowledge, thus preparing the soil for agnosticism. Herein lies its difference from theosophy. Theosophy takes greater account of the irrational and mysterious nature of things divine, and allows more freely the possibility of an infinite evolution in the knowledge of these mysteries, while rejecting, on the other hand, conceptual knowledge. Theology prefers to use concepts—especially Catholic school theology, which has been worked out to such perfection.

The following concept of rational, cataphatic theology is what I call comedy: God, it would seem, the perfect and unmoving, complete, satisfied, all-powerful, all-knowing, and infinitely good God has created the world and man for His own glory and for the good of creation. The act of the creation of the world has not been prompted by anything, did not answer any need of God, but was the result of a purely and simply arbitrary decision—it added nothing to the Divine Being, enriched it in no way. God endowed man, His creature, with the fatal faculty of freedom, saw in freedom a privilege of His creation and an image of Himself. Yet man made bad use of this freedom, joined in a rebellion against his creator, fell away from God, and in his fall dragged with him all creation. Man, who violated the will of God, became subject to damnation and to the power of the Law. All creation groans and weeps. End of the first act.

With the second act begins the redemption that took place in the incarnation of the Son of God who wished to save created man. The person of the Creator is relegated to the shadows, in favor of the person of the Redemptor. Still it must be noted that all this cosmology and anthropology is constructed according to the principle of integral monotheism, without the least reference to Christ and *before* the revelation of the Holy Trinity. We are dealing here with a dualistic theism that knows nothing of the Divine Trinity, knows only the monarchic doctrine of God—a doctrine, that is, which has in it nothing Christian. The comedy of God's game with himself lies in the fact that God, endowing man with freedom, could not in His omnipotence foresee what consequences this freedom would bring in its train: sin, evil, cosmic suffering and pain, eternal damnation and tortures of Hell no less eternal, for an undetermined and obviously large number of beings created for God's good. Man appears as a plaything without importance, who receives his freedom from outside and upon whom is laid at the same time a responsibility beyond his means. He is great only in his fall.

For God all is accomplished in eternity and in the act of the creation of the world, while in eternity all suffering, temporal and eternal, is predestined. This leads inevitably to the doctrine that some are predestined for salvation, others to eternal loss—a doctrine towards which even St. Augustine inclined and which Calvin drew out to its last consequence. God who created the world predetermined its eternal loss, for he knew the consequences of freedom, knew what man's choice would be. Man has received freedom from God, not from himself, and this freedom is exclusively under the power of God, totally determined by Him—that is, it is ultimately a fiction. God invites the creature to love God and begin a divine life, but God expects an answer only from Himself, for it is He who gives freedom and knows the consequences of freedom. The problem of Ivan Karamazov is worked out more fully and transposed into eternity.

What is at stake is not the tears of a child in time and on earth, but the suffering, temporal and eternal, of a vast number of living creatures who have received from God the fatal gift of freedom—God knowing the meaning and consequences of this gift. The soteriology of the traditional theological systems can easily be interpreted as a reparation, unworthy of God, of the fault he himself committed, a reparation which at the same time takes the form of correction. Rational cataphatic theology, forgetful in its cosmology and anthropology of the Divine Trinity and of Christ, God of love and sacrifice, and ascribing the mystery of Christian revelation to the redemption rather than the creation of the world, cannot get beyond this stage of divine comedy, and constructs a fictitious theodicy. The theological doctrine of free will has an educational, moral-juridical character, but does not penetrate the first mystery of freedom. It exists only to punish. In such a view, apophatic and cataphatic elements are hopelessly mixed up.

Jacob Boehme was one of those rare people with the hardihood to go beyond such rational and cataphatic theology, and to conceive of the mystery of the creation of the world not as a comedy but as a tragedy. He speaks not merely of a cosmogonic or anthropogonic process, but also of a theogonic process. But "theogony" does not mean that God had a beginning and was born in time; Boehme did not mean, as did Fichte and Hegel, that God is born within a temporal process, but that God's interior and eternal life manifests itself under the form of a dynamic process, of tragedy within eternity, of battle against the darkness of nonbeing. The doctrine of the Unground and of freedom is a bold attempt to understand the creation of the world through the inner life of the divinity. The creation of the world is part of the interior life of the Divine Trinity and it can be for the Divine Trinity something absolutely exterior. In this way the principle of evil becomes tragic. Boehme's cosmogony and anthropology are steeped in Christian revelation, they do not remain captives of the Old Testament, they are bathed in the light of the New Testament, the light of Christ. Boehme tells us of the terrible "suffering of the Unground" which the light of Christ must surmount.

III

Boehme's doctrine of the Unground does not at once take its definitive form. We do not find it in *Aurora*. It is developed mainly in *De Signatura Rerum* and in *Mysterium Magnum*. It responds to Boehme's need to grasp the mysteries of freedom, the origin of evil, and the battle between light and darkness. In the third chapter of *De Signatura Rerum*, entitled "Of the Great Mystery of All Things," Boehme says: "Taken out of nature, God is a Mystery, that is, in Nothingness; for outside of nature there is Nothing— an eye of eternity, an unfathomable eye which resides in and looks into nothing, because it is the Unground; and this eye is a will, a desire of manifestation to find Nothingness." The Unground, thus, is nothingness, the unfathomable eye of eternity and at the same time a will, a will without bottom, abysmal, indeterminate. But it is a nothingness which is "the hunger for Something." At the same time the Unground is "Freedom." In the darkness of the Unground blaze the flames signifying freedom, meontic, potential freedom. According to Boehme, freedom is nature's counterpart, while nature has issued from freedom. Freedom resembles nothingness, but it is out of freedom that something has come. The hunger for freedom, the motiveless hunger for something must be stilled. "Nothingness appears in the darkness of death in its desire to issue from freedom, for Nothing cannot and will not be Nothing." The freedom of the Unground is neither light nor darkness, nor good, nor evil. Freedom resides in darkness and is thirsting for light. And freedom is the cause of light. "Freedom is and resides in darkness, it turns away from the desire for darkness toward the desire for light, it seizes the darkness with its eternal will; and darkness tries to seize the light of freedom and cannot attain it, for darkness closes in again upon itself with its desires, and transforms itself back into darkness."

Apophatically and antinomically, Boehme describes the mystery that takes place in the depths of being, in that depth which touches upon first nothingness. In the darkness, the fire blazes and the light glimmers, nothing becomes something, unfathomable freedom produces nature. And two processes take place: "Freedom is the cause of light, and the pressure of desire is the cause of darkness and painful suffering. Understand these as two beginnings, that is, as two principles: the one which resides in freedom and light, the other which resides in the pressure, pain, and suffering of darkness; and each resides within itself. . . . Freedom, Nothingness, has in itself no essence." Boehme was perhaps the first man in the history of human thought to recognize that the foundations of being, prior to being, are unfathomable freedom, the passionate desire of nothing to become something, the darkness in which fire and light are burning; in other words, he was the founder of an original metaphysical voluntarism that is unknown to medieval and classical thought.

According to Boehme, will—freedom—is the principle of all things. But Boehme holds that the Unground, the unfathomable will, resides in the depths of divinity and before divinity. The Unground is the divinity of apophatic theology, and is at the same time the abyss, the free nothingness which extends below God and beyond God. In God there is nature

which is a principle different from Him. The first
divinity, divine nothingness, is beyond good and evil,
beyond light and darkness. The divine Unground
exists in eternity before the birth of the Divine
Trinity. God is engendered, is realized out of divine
nothingness. This road, plunging into divine wisdom,
is akin to that by which Meister Eckhardt distinguished between divinity and God. God as creator of
the world and of man is correlative to creation. He
surges from the depths of divinity, the inexpressible
nothing. Such is the deepest and most secret idea of
German mysticism.

This road which plunges into divine wisdom is ir-
revocably determined by apophatic theology. Everything that Boehme says about the divine Unground
belongs to apophatic and not to cataphatic theology.
Nothingness is deeper than and prior to something.
Darkness (which is not yet evil) is deeper than and
prior to light, freedom is deeper than and prior to all
nature. The God of cataphatic theology is already a
something, a thought about a secondary phenomenon.
*"The reason for this 'tincture' is divine wisdom, and the
reason for the wisdom is the Trinity of the Indeterminate
Divinity, and the reason for the Indeterminate Divinity
is the unfathomable will, and the reason for the will is
Nothingness."* All this is none other than the theogonic process, the process of the birth of God in eternity in the eternal mystery which is described according to the methods of apophatic theology. And this
is precisely why this thought is less heretical than it
might seem to the extreme partisans of cataphatic—
rationalized—theology. Boehme's process of contemplation is more profound than all the affirmations of

secondary and rationalized cataphasis. Boehme upholds the legitimacy of the way which leads "from the
eternal reason of nature, the free will of the Unground,
toward the natural reason of the soul." According to
him, nature is always a secondary and derivative
phenomenon. Freedom, will are not nature. Freedom
has not been created. "When I consider what God is,
I say: He is the One, face to face with the creature,
that is, an eternal Nothing; He has neither reason nor
beginning nor abode; He possesses nothing but Himself; He is the will of the Unground; He is but one
thing in Himself: He needs no space nor place; He is
engendered in Himself from eternity to eternity; He
is not similar to or identical with anything and He
resides in no particular place; His abode is eternal
wisdom or intelligence; He is the will of wisdom, wisdom is His manifestation."

The Unground must first of all be considered as
freedom, as freedom in darkness. "This is why the
eternal and free will has entered into darkness, suffering, and pain, and through darkness into fire and
light and a realm of delights: so that the Nothing
might be known in the Something and might play
with its counterpart, so that the free will of the Unground might manifest itself in the motive, for without Evil and without Good there could be no reason."
The roots of freedom descend into nothing, into the
me on, freedom is the Unground. "Free will has no
beginning stemming from a reason; it has not been
formed by anything. . . . Its true origin is in Nothingness. . . . Further, free will has within itself its own
judgment of Good and Evil, has its judgment within
itself, has within itself the anger and the love of God."

Free will has within it also darkness and light. Free will in God is the Unground in God, nothingness within him.

Boehme gives a profound interpretation of the truth of freedom in God, which is also recognized by traditional Christian theology. His teaching of the freedom of God is more profound than that of Duns Scotus! "The eternal intelligence of the divinity is a free will neither born from nor engendered by Something, it is its own abode and resides purely and simply within itself, incapable of being grasped by anything, for outside of it and prior to it nothing exists and this Nothing is one and yet is like itself only a Nothing. The divine intelligence is a unique will of the Unground, is neither far nor near, neither high nor low, but is everything—and yet appears as a Nothing." To Boehme, chaos is the root of nature, chaos meaning freedom, the Unground, the will, the irrational principle. Within divinity itself there is an indeterminate will, that is, an irrational principle. Darkness and freedom are in Boehme constantly related and associated. Freedom itself is God, and was at the beginning of all things. "Thus we can rightly say that it belongs to God and that freedom (which possesses will) is God Himself since it is eternity and nothing else. First of all there is eternal will, which possesses will and which itself is will." Boehme, first in the history of human thought, has made freedom the first foundation of being, freedom is to him deeper and more primary than all being, deeper and more primary than God Himself.

The consequences for the history of thought have been considerable. Such a view of the originality of

freedom would have startled the Greek philosophers
no less than the medieval Scholastics. The possibility
of an entirely different theodicy and an entirely different anthropodicy is now open. The first mystery
of being is a sudden illumination of dark freedom, of
nothingness, a solidification of the world from this
dark freedom. Boehme speaks about it in a magnificent passage in his *Psychologia Vera:* "For in the
darkness appears the lightning, and in freedom appears light with majesty. And this is but the separation that renders darkness material, the darkness in
which clearly no conceivable being exists; but a dark
spirit and force, an accomplishment of the will within
itself—within and not outside of the desire, for outside the desire there is freedom."

There exist two wills—the one in fire, the other in
light. Fire and light are the basic symbols of Boehme:
"For the darkness conceals a fire that is cold until
fear reaches it; then it blazes and burns." Fire is the
principle of everything, without fire nothing would
exist, there would be nothing but the Unground.
"Everything would be Nothingness and Unground if
there were no fire." The transition from nonbeing to
being is achieved by the fire blazing out of freedom.
In eternity there is the primitive will of the Unground,
the will that is outside of and prior to nature. Fichte
and Hegel, Schopenhauer and Hartmann stem from
here, even though they dechristianize Boehme. Idealist German metaphysics comes directly from the Unground, the Un-conscient, it proceeds from the primitive act of freedom to the process of the world—not
to the Divine Trinity, as it does with Boehme. The
first mystery of being consists, according to Boehme,

in the fact that nothing feels a passion for something. "The Unground is an eternal Nothing but it gives an eternal beginning, that is, a passion; for the Nothing is a passion for Something. But nothing exists that produces something; but there is the passion which gives itself, and which yet is nothing else than a simple passion directed toward itself." In Boehme, the doctrine of freedom is not a psychological and ethical doctrine of the freedom of will, but a metaphysical doctrine of the Unground of being. Freedom is for him not the justification of man's moral responsibility, nor the normalization of man's relation with God and his neighbor, but an explanation of the genesis of being and, at the same time, of the genesis of evil as an ontological and cosmological problem.

For Boehme, evil stems from evil imagination. The magic of imagination plays a considerable part in Boehme's philosophy. By imagination the world was created, and by it the fall of the Devil in the universe was brought about. The fall of the creature is, in Boehme's view, decided not in the human world but in the world of angels; the human world did not appear until afterward and was to repair the act committed by the fallen angel. Here is how Boehme defines the fall of Lucifer: "For Lucifer abandoned the repose of his command to fall into eternal restlessness." There followed a displacement of the hierarchical center, a violation of the hierarchical order. And elsewhere, Boehme described the fall of Lucifer thus: "Free will gazed upon itself in the fiery mirror and saw what it was, and this radiance animated it, so that it became animated toward the properties of the Centrum which at once began to produce qualities.

For the biting and hard desire, that is, the first form or property, received its imprint and awakened the good and the anxious desire; thus this beautiful star darkened its light and became pungent, rude, and hard; and its sweetness and its wholly angelic property transformed themselves into a being altogether hard, rude, and dark: this is what became of the beautiful morning star, and its legions followed suit; such is the fall." The fall comes from dark aspiration, from desire, from the evil imagination of dark magic.

Boehme always describes the fall in a mythological manner, never by clear concepts. Desire calls forth burning pain in the Devil lost in his darkness. Without Boehme's doctrine concerning the Unground and freedom, the source of original sin and of evil is incomprehensible. Original sin and evil are for Boehme cosmic catastrophies, a moment in the creation of the world, in the cosmogonic and anthropogonic process, the result of the strife between opposing properties, darkness and light, anger and love. The catastrophies precede the birth of our world; before our aeon there were others. Evil has besides a positive sense within the birth of the cosmos and of man. Evil is the shadow of good—light presupposes the existence of darkness. Light, the good, love need their opposite principles to become manifest—a counterpart, a *Gegenwurf*. God Himself shows two faces, the face of love and the face of wrath, a face of light and a face of darkness. "For the God of the sacred world and the God of the dark world are not two different Gods: there is only one God; He Himself is all Being, He is Evil and Good, heaven and hell, light and darkness, eternity and time, the beginning and the end; wherever His love be-

comes hidden in a being there appears His wrath."
And he continues: "The force that is in the light is the
fire of God's love, and the force that is in the darkness
is the fire of His wrath, and yet there is only one fire,
which yet divides itself in two principles, so that the
one may appear in the other. For the flame of wrath
is the manifestation of great love; in the darkness one
knows the light, else light could not become manifest
to itself." Boehme is the originator of this brilliant
doctrine according to which the love of God, in dark
surroundings, transforms itself into anger, into wrath,
and recognizes itself as such.

Boehme always thinks in antitheses. To him all life
is fire but fire manifests itself doubly. "There are two
eternal lives, two different sources, and each resides
within its fire. The one burns in love and the realm
of delights. The other in wrath, anger, and pain, and
its materials are pride, greed, envy, and wrath; its
force is like a sulphurous spirit. For the rise of pride
and greed, envy and anger are a brimstone in which
the fire burns, and where it blazes always feeding on
this matter. . . . Christ on the cross has to absorb
into his secret and divine Being this angry wrath that
has awakened in the essence of Adam, and through
his great love to transform it into heavenly delights."
Boehme conceives redemption cosmogonically and an-
thropogonically as an extension of the creation of the
world.

Schelling, in his *Philosophical Inquiry into the Essence of Human Freedom*, comes close to the ideas of
Boehme on freedom and the Unground, although he
does not always understand Boehme exactly. The following words of Schelling recall Boehme very closely:

"Every birth is a birth that draws from obscurity to bring into light." According to Schelling, the first creation is the birth of light, dominion over darkness. Freedom, he says, is indispensable to the good if it is to pass from darkness, from potentiality to actuality. To Schelling, being is will. First in German philosophy, he develops the voluntarism of Boehme. Things have their basis not in God Himself, but in the nature of God. Evil is possible only because there is within God something that is not God, because there is in God a dark will, in other words, the Unground. To Schelling, as to Boehme, nature is the history of the spirit; and for Schelling, everything that is perceived in nature, in the objective world, passes through the subject. The idea of process within God, the idea of theogony, Schelling borrowed from Boehme.

In his *Philosophy of Revelation* Schelling makes an heroic effort to overcome German idealism and to reach a philosophical realism. Here Boehme is of great help to him. Schelling tried to overcome the pantheistic monism of German idealist philosophy. He recognized that pantheism is incompatible with freedom. The pantheistic denial of evil leads to the denial of freedom. Evil, says Schelling, has its roots in that which is the most positive of all things. Evil is the lack of the root of existence, that is, it is linked to the Unground, to potential freedom. All this, of course, is Boehme. Yet closer to Boehme, and more kindred to his genius, seems to us Franz von Baader, the mind least corrupted by the idealists' break with being, who led Schelling to Boehme. Baader was a Catholic, though very free in his Catholicism and very sympathetic to Eastern orthodoxy. With perfect clarity and simplicity, Baader justifies Boehme's dynamic concept of God, a concept which admits of a genesis within the divine life. If there were no genesis in the consciousness God has of Himself, this consciousness would not know either life or process. The dynamic concept of God means in effect that for us God is living and animated, and that at the base of the divine life there is the tragic that pertains to all life. All this may not be in accord with St. Thomas Aquinas and Scholastic theology, but in any event it corresponds with biblical revelation. Still, Baader gives us an excellent definition of evil as a sickness, a distortion of the hierarchical order, a displacement of the center of being which causes being to pass into nonbeing.

IV

It is characteristic of the philosophy of Boehme that he hated the idea of predestination. In this matter, he lacked the Protestant spirit (as Koyré in particular has stressed). He wished to defend the goodness of God and the freedom of man, both of which were sapped by the doctrine of predestination. He was ready to sacrifice the omnipotence and omniscience of God, and to admit that God had not foreseen the consequences of freedom. He said that God had not foreseen the fall of the angels. This problem tormented him greatly, and his torment constitutes the moral importance of his creative way. But on this point Boehme is not always in agreement with himself, his thought is antinomical, at times even contradictory. His originality lies in his antinomical attitude toward evil. From this point of view he shows a certain similarity to Dostoevsky.

The evil which tormented Boehme so greatly finds an explanation in the fact that the primitive foundation of being is the unmotivated, dark, irrational, meontic freedom, a potentiality which nothing can determine. For Boehme, dark freedom is impenetrable to God; God does not foresee its consequences and is not responsible for the evil that comes from it, since freedom was not created by God. The doctrine of the Unground unburdens God of the responsibility for an evil provoked by divine omniscience and omnipotence. At the same time, Boehme perceives the Unground in God Himself; there is in God a dark principle, the battle of light and darkness. One could say that the dark principle ("dark" does not here mean "evil") resides not in God but in divinity. In a truly extreme manner, Boehme opposes the face of the Son, which is the face of love, to the face of the Father, which is anger. There is in the Son already no dark principle, he is all light, all love, all goodness. But the Father then takes the form of a divinity of apophatic theology. Gnostic motifs here become discernible. But the evil that torments Boehme so greatly has for him also a positive mission. The divine light can manifest itself only through the counterpart of something other, something opposed—darkness. Such is the case with all actualization, all genesis. Evil is not only a negative principle, it is also a positive principle. Yet evil at the same time always remains evil which must be consumed, overcome. Nowhere in nature is there calmness, eternal order—everywhere there is the conflict of opposing principles. And this conflict of opposing principles retains a positive meaning. Only through this conflict are the highest life, the good, and love made manifest. Being is a reunion of contraries, of *Yes* and *No*. *Yes* remains impossible without *No*. All being, and divinity itself, consists of a fiery movement —and this does not mean, as nineteenth-century German idealist metaphysics would have it, that God is only a God in the state of becoming, an ideal limit of the universal process.

Being is the victory over nonbeing. For Boehme there is a hell, but for him as for Swedenborg that hell does not imply suffering. Boehme had already that new soul which could no longer say, with St. Thomas Aquinas, that the just man in Paradise rejoices at the sight of the torments of sinners in hell. Boehme's ideas on freedom and the Unground remain antinomical. Since they have grown from his intuition of the Unground, they lack concordance and logical consistency. When German idealist metaphysics attempted to lend them this logical concordance and consistency, it found itself unable to overcome the tragic antinomy of evil and freedom within the supreme consciousness; it suppressed that antinomy, and by this monism lost the edge of the original, sharp, burning feeling of evil and freedom. Boehme's doctrine of the Unground explains through freedom the origin of evil, the fall of Lucifer, who drew down with him every creature; at the same time, the Unground is introduced into God Himself and explains the genesis, the dynamic process in the divine life. There appears here the possibility of slipping toward extreme monism, and toward a no less extreme dualism which, from the point of view of Christian revelation, would be equally mistaken. Boehme's thought moves constantly on the razor's edge, constantly courting dangers on either side. But his basic intuition is that of a genius, organic and fertile. The doctrine of the Unground and of freedom resists the Hellenic rationalism in which medieval Scholasticism was steeped, and of which even patristics were not free.

We must salute Boehme as the founder of that philosophy of freedom which represents the true Christian philosophy. The anti-tragic and rationalist optimism of St. Thomas Aquinas gives way to the tragic philosophy of freedom. Freedom is the source of tragedy. Hegel attempted to endow the principle of contradiction and of the conflict of opposing principles with an optimistic character. He transformed light into a concept, and made of the concept itself the source of drama and the passions. Hegel, after St. Thomas Aquinas, represents the second brilliant rise of rationalism. But Hegel's philosophy rests upon an irrational base. His divinity is at its source an unconscient divinity, and only in human philosophy, in the philosophy of Hegel himself, does it achieve consciousness. The irrational must be rationalized, light must arise in the darkness. The rational knowledge of the irrational that is at the base of being is the magnificent basic theme of German metaphysics. German philosophy represents the metaphysical North. The world is not from the beginning and naturally illumined by the light of the sun, but is plunged in darkness, light is produced by a penetration into the subject from the depths of the spirit. That is the fundamental difference between Latin thought and Germanic thought. Germanic thought conceives reason other than does Latin thought. In Germanic thought, reason faces the darkness of the irrational into which it must bring light. In Latin thought, as in the thought of antiquity, reason illumined the world from the very beginning, like the sun, and reason in man is a reflection of the reason which is in the nature of things. The Germanic idea stems from Boehme, from the doctrine of the Unground and of freedom, from the irrational principle which is at the root of being. With Boehme a new era in the history of Christian thought begins. His influence is considerable but unobtrusive. Apparently manifest only in Franz von Baader and Schelling, it makes itself equally felt in Fichte, Hegel, and Schopenhauer.

Strong also is Boehme's influence on romanticism and occultist currents. Without his brilliant intuitions, the rationalism of modern philosophy, of Descartes and Spinoza, could not have been overcome. Mythological thought alone perceived the irrational principle within being, while philosophical thought saw only the rational principle. Boehme leads metaphysics back to the sources of the mythological consciousness of mankind. This mythological consciousness, in Boehme, draws its own nourishment from the sources of biblical revelation. Boehme is the fountainhead of the dynamism of German philosophy, one might even say of the dynamism of the entire thought of the nineteenth century. He was the first to conceive cosmic life as an impassioned battle, as a movement, as a process, as an eternal genesis. Only such an intuition of cosmic life made possible the "Faust," made possible Darwin, Marx, Nietzsche, men who were already far removed from Boehme's religious considerations.

Boehme's doctrine of the Unground and of freedom

not only allows us to explain the origin of evil, however antinomical it may be, it also explains the creative power of the new in cosmic life, the creative dynamism. By its nature, creative power has issued from meontic freedom, from nothingness, from the Unground, it presupposes within being this unfathomable source, it presupposes that darkness must be illuminated. But Boehme's singularity lies in his seeing the Unground, the dark principle, within God Himself, rather than perceiving the principle of freedom in nothingness, in the *me on*, outside of God. According to him, we must distinguish between the divine nothingness, and the nonbeing outside of God. It would be wrong, however, to interpret Boehme's philosophy in a gross manner. Boehme would not have been willing to see in God the source of evil. This precisely is the point that tortured him. His thought remains antinomical, it does not suffer logical commentary. But his moral will remains pure, not for a moment has it been corrupted by the evil within. Boehme is a devout Christian, endowed with a burning faith and a pure heart. In him, the prudence of the serpent is paired with simplicity of heart, with faith. We must never forget this when judging Boehme. He is neither a pantheist nor a monist, any more than he is a Manichaean. Carriere was right when he said that Boehme was neither a pantheist nor a dualist.

German philosophy of identity—which had lost touch with the sources of Christian revelation, of Christian realism—not only developed Boehme's idea of the Unground, it also deformed it. That is how German metaphysics began to turn toward impersonalism and monism, and to teach that God is a "becoming" in the cosmic process. Nonetheless his voluntarism proved most fruitful for philosophy: this is clearly true of his doctrine of the conflict of opposing principles, of light and darkness, and of the need for a counterpart by which positive principles could become manifest. Boehme's metaphysics is a musical and Christian metaphysics, and thus highly characteristic of the German spirit. Herein lies the difference that separates it from the architectonic Christian metaphysics of St. Thomas Aquinas, characteristic of the Latin spirit. The German metaphysicians of the nineteenth century attempted to express a musical theme by means of a system of concepts. This is the greatness of their attempt, this is also the reason for the failure of those systems.

Today, a Boehme renaissance is not impossible. Many books are being written about him. He could help us to overcome not only the routines of Greek and medieval Scholastic thought, but also the German idealism which he himself influenced from within. To us Russians, Boehme and von Baader certainly seem much closer than any other Western thinker. Our spiritual qualities impose upon us a mission of constructing a philosophy of tragedy, because the optimistic rationalism of European thought is alien to us. Boehme so loved freedom that he could see the true Church only where there was freedom. He influenced Russian mystical currents of the end of the eighteenth and the beginning of the nineteenth centuries, but he was appropriated naively and without creative rethinking. He was translated into Russian, and brought to a wide public that venerated him almost as a Father of the Church. It is an interesting fact that

Alexander Herzen, in his *Letters on the Study of Nature*, spoke of Boehme with enthusiasm. We later find Boehme's influence in Soloviev, though here it is overlaid with a rationalist scheme. Soloviev's philosophy cannot be considered a philosophy of freedom and of tragedy. Nonetheless, in Russian thought of the beginning of this century, Soloviev is the author of lines that come closest to Boehme.

The guardians of orthodoxy who take a special pleasure in unmasking heresies fear the influence of Boehme as that of a heterodox, a protestant, a gnostic, and a theosophist. But is not all Western thought outside of orthodoxy? From that point of view, one would have to avoid all contact with Western thought, and oppose it as a snare and a delusion. That would of course be the purest obscurantism, the ambition to return to our ancient poverty of thought. Did not the Christian world, in its most creative period, feed on the pagan thought of antiquity? In any case, Boehme was more Christian than Plato, who, obedient to patristic tradition, is highly honored among us, more Christian especially than Kant, who is venerated by many orthodox theologians. Boehme is very hard to understand, and it is possible to draw from his work the most varied, if not the most contradictory, conclusions. To me Boehme's importance for Christian philosophy and Christian theosophy lies in his efforts to break, by his vision, the powerful hold of Greco-Latin thought upon the Christian conscience, and in his penetration of the first mystery of life which the thought of antiquity concealed. Christian theology (and not only Catholic theology) is so deeply imbued with Greek thought, Platonism, Aristotelianism, and Stoicism, that an attack upon this manner of thinking appears like an attack upon Christian revelation. Were not the Greek doctors of the Church disciples of Greek philosophy, were they not Platonists? Their thought retained the imprint of the limits of Greek rationalism. It did not succeed in solving the problem of personality, the problem of freedom, the problem of creative dynamism.

Boehme not only is no Aristotelian, he is no Platonist. His influence escapes the conflict that pits Eastern Platonism against Western Aristotelianism. The only thinker to whom he is close is Heraclitus. I do not think that it is necessary for Christian philosophy to conquer both Platonism and Aristotelianism, static philosophies that divide the world and are unable to seize the secrets of freedom and of creative power. Boehme's doctrine of the "Sophia," of divine wisdom, is not Christian Platonism. Its meaning is altogether different. Still the doctrine of the Unground and of freedom must be developed—the distinction between the divine abyss and divine freedom, and the distinction between the meontic abyss and meontic freedom. It is in this last inexpressible mystery that the difference will disappear. But the distinction is inevitable for those who still stand on the threshold of this mystery.

CONTENTS

SIX THEOSOPHIC POINTS

ON THE DIVINE INTUITION

SEX PUNCTA THEOSOPHICA

OR

HIGH AND DEEP GROUNDING OF

SIX THEOSOPHIC POINTS

AN OPEN GATE OF ALL THE SECRETS OF LIFE
WHEREIN THE CAUSES OF ALL BEINGS
BECOME KNOWN

Written in the year 1620

AUTHOR'S PREFACE TO THE READER

WE have written this work, not for the irrational animals who, in their exterior, have the form of man, but in their image, in spirit, are evil and wild beasts, which is disclosed and exhibited by their properties; but for the image of man, for those who are budding forth out of the animal image with a human image that belongs to God's kingdom, and who would fain live and grow in the human image, in the right man. Those who are often and much hindered by the contrarious life, and thus are involved in the mixed life, and travail in desire for the birth of the holy life : for them are these writings written. And we bid them not regard it as impossible to discern and to know such mystery ; and we give them this to consider of in a similitude. Let them imagine a life which is the outcome and growth of all lives, and is mixed. But let them also imagine another life to grow in it from all the lives, which, though it had grown from all the lives, was free from all the other lives, and yet possessed all the essential properties of those lives. This other new life (let them imagine) is illuminated with the light, and only in itself ; so that it could behold all the other lives, and they (the other lives) could not see nor apprehend the new life. Thus is every one, who, out of the mixed life, evil and good, is born again in and of God. This new image, born in the life of God, beholds all the natural lives, and nothing is strange or difficult to it; for it beholds only its root from which it grew. As a fair flower grows out of the rough earth, which is not like the earth but declares by its beauty the power of the earth, and how it is mixed of good and evil; so also is every man, who, out of the animal, wild, earthly nature and quality, is born again so as to become the right image of God.

For those who are a growth of such a kind, and are shooting forth into the fair lily in the kingdom of God, and are in process of birth, have we written this book; that they should strengthen their essences therein, bud in the life of God, and grow and bear fruit in the tree of paradise. And seeing all the children of God grow in this tree, and each is a twig of this same tree, we have wished to impart to our twigs and fellow-branches in our tree, in which we all are, and from which we all grow, our sap, savour and essence, that our tree of paradise may become great, and that we may rejoice one with another. And we would urge all children, who are thus growing in this tree, friendly to ponder that each branch and twig helps to shelter the other from the storm, and we commend ourselves unto their love and growth.

THE FIRST POINT

CHAPTER I

*Of the first growth and life from the first Principle.
That we are so to ponder and consider it, as if it
stood alone and were not mixed with the other,—
what its power might be. That, therefore, we
are not to think of it as being such that it is one
and united in a single figure or creation; but
[we are to think of it so] that we learn to explore
and fathom the* centrum naturae, *and to distinguish the divine Essence from Nature.*

1. We see and find that every life is essential,
and find moreover that it is based on will; for will
is the driving of the essences.

2. It is thus, as if a hidden fire lay in the will,
and the will continually uplifting itself towards the
fire wished to awaken and kindle it.

3. For we understand that every will without
the awakening of the fiery essences is an impotency,
as it were dumb without life, wherein is no feeling,
understanding nor substantiality. It resembles

only a shadow without substance ; for it has no conductor, but sinks down and suffers itself to be driven and led like a dead thing,—such as is to be compared to a shadow, which is led along without essence.

4. Thus an unessential will is a dumb existence without comprehension or life ; and yet is a figure in the unfathomable eternal nothing, for it is attached to the corporeal things.

5. Now, as the will without essence is dumb and without being, so in the essence it is a being and image according to the essences, which is fashioned after the essences ; for the life of the will is generated from the essences.

6. Thus life is the essences' son, and the will, wherein life's figure stands, is the essences' father ; for no essence can arise without will. For in the will is originated desire, in which the essences take their rise.

7. Seeing then the first will is an ungrounded-ness, to be regarded as an eternal nothing, we recognize it to be like a mirror, wherein one sees his own image ; like a life, and yet it is no life, but a figure of life and of the image belonging to life.

8. Thus we recognize the eternal Unground out of Nature to be like a mirror. For it is like an eye which sees, and yet conducts nothing in the seeing wherewith it sees ; for seeing is without essence, although it is generated from essence, viz. from the essential life.

9. We are able then to recognize that the eternal Unground out of Nature is a will, like an eye where-in Nature is hidden ; like a hidden fire that burns

not, which exists and also exists not. It is not a spirit, but a form of spirit, like the reflection in the mirror. For all the form of a spirit is seen in the reflection or in the mirror, and yet there is nothing which the eye or mirror sees; but its seeing is in itself, for there is nothing before it that were deeper there. It is like a mirror which is a container of the aspect of Nature, and yet comprehends not Nature, as Nature comprehends not the form of the image in the mirror.

10. And thus one is free from the other, and yet the mirror is truly the container of the image. It embraces the image, and yet is powerless in respect of the form, for it cannot retain it. For if the image depart from the mirror, the mirror is a clear brightness, and its brightness is a nothing; and yet all the form of Nature is hidden therein as a nothing; and yet veritably is, but not in essence.

11. And so it is to be understood concerning the hidden eternal wisdom of God, which resembles an eternal eye without essence. It is the unground, and yet sees all; all has been hidden in it from eternity, and therefrom it has its seeing. But it is not essential, as in the mirror the brightness is not essential, which yet embraces all that appears before it.

12. Secondly, this is to be understood also of the eternal will, which likewise is without essence, as also of the Spirit of God. For no seeing is without spirit, neither is any spirit without seeing. And we understand thus, that seeing shines forth from the spirit, and is its eye or mirror, wherein the will is revealed. For seeing makes a will, as the

unground of the deep without number knows to find
no ground nor limit; hence its mirror goeth into
itself, and makes a ground in itself, that is a will.

13. Thus the mirror of the eternal eye shines
forth in the will, and generates to itself another
eternal ground within itself. This is its centre or
heart, from which the seeing continually takes its
rise from eternity, and through which the will becomes moving and directive, namely of that which
the centre brings forth.

14. For all is comprised in the will, and is an
essence, which, in the eternal Unground, eternally
takes its rise in itself, enters into itself, grasps
itself in itself, and makes the centre in itself; but
with that which is grasped passes out of itself,
manifests itself in the brightness of the eye, and
thus shines forth out of the essence in itself and
from itself. It is its own, and yet also in comparison to Nature is as a nothing (understand,
in comparison to palpable being, so to speak);
though it is all, and all arises from thence.

15. And herein we understand the eternal Essence of the triad of the Deity, with the unfathomable wisdom. For the eternal will, which
comprehends the eye or the mirror, wherein lies
the eternal seeing as its wisdom, is Father. And
that which is eternally grasped in wisdom, the
grasp comprehending a basis or centre in itself,
passing out of the ungroundedness into a ground,
is Son or Heart; for it is the Word of life, or its
essentiality, in which the will shines forth with
lustre.

16. And the going within itself to the centre of

the ground is Spirit ; for it is the finder, who from eternity continually finds where there is nothing. It goes forth again from the centre of the ground, and seeks in the will. And then the mirror of the eye, viz. the Father's and Son's wisdom, becomes manifest ; and wisdom stands accordingly before the Spirit of God, who in it manifests the unground. For its virtue, wherein the colours of the wonders shine forth, is revealed from the Father of the eternal will through the centre of his Heart or Ground by the forthgoing Spirit.

17. For it (wisdom) is that which is uttered, which the Father utters out of the centre of the Heart by the Holy Spirit, and stands in divine forms and images, in the ocular view of the Holy Tri-unity of God; but as a virgin without bringing forth. It generates not the colours and figures which shine forth in it, and are revealed in the ground and essence ; but all is together an eternal *Magia*, and dwells with the centre of the heart in itself, and by the spirit goes forth from the centre out of itself, and manifests itself in the eye of virgin wisdom endlessly.

18. For as the essence of the Deity has no ground from which it arises or proceeds, so also the Will-spirit has no ground where it might rest, where there were a place or limit, but it is called Wonderful. And its word or heart, from which it goes forth, is called the eternal Power of the Deity ; and the will which generates the heart and the power in itself is called eternal Counsel.

19. Thus the essence of the Deity is everywhere in the deep of the unground, like as a wheel or eye,

where the beginning hath always the end; and there is no place found for it, for it is itself the place of all beings and the fulness of all things, and yet is apprehended or seen by nothing. For it is an eye in itself, as Ezekiel the prophet saw this in a figure at the introduction of the spirit of his will into God, when his spiritual figure was introduced into the wisdom of God by the Spirit of God; there he attained the vision, and in no other way can that be.

The Second Text.

20. We understand, then, that the divine Essence in threefoldness in the unground dwells in itself, but generates to itself a ground within itself, viz. the eternal word or heart, which is the centre or goal of rest in the Deity; though this is not to be understood as to being, but as to a threefold spirit, where each is the cause of the birth of the other.

21. And this threefold spirit is not measurable, divisible or fathomable; for there is no place found for it, and it is at the same time the unground of eternity, which gives birth to itself within itself in a ground. And no place or position can be conceived or found where the spirit of the tri-unity is not present, and in every being; but hidden to the being, dwelling in itself, as an essence that at once fills all and yet dwells not in being, but itself has a being in itself; as we are to reflect concerning the ground and unground, how the two are to be understood in reference to each other.

22. Thus, we understand eternity: (1) How it

was before the times of the creation of this world.
(2) What the divine Essence is in itself without a
principle. (3) What the eternal beginning in the
unground is, and the eternal end in its own ground
generated in itself, viz. the centre to the word,
which word is the centre itself. (4) And yet the
eternal birth of the Word in the will, in the mirror
of the eternal wisdom, in the virgin, continually
takes place from eternity to eternity without a
genetrix or without bringing forth.

23. And in this virgin of the wisdom of God
the eternal principle is as a hidden fire, which is
recognized as in a mirror by its colours. It has
been known from eternity to eternity in figure, and
is known also thus to all eternity in the eternal
origin, in wisdom.

24. And in this mirror, where the principle is
disclosed from the eternal Unground, the essence
of the three principles, according to the likeness of
the holy triad, has been seen with their wonders as
in an unfathomable deep, and that from eternity.

25. We are now to understand that the first
Principle is magical in origin ; for it is generated in
desire, in the will. Hence its craving and contra-
will to bring forth is also magical, namely to bring
forth the second Principle.

26. And whereas in the first and second principle
only a spirit without comprehensible [corporeal]
being is understood ; yet there is also the craving
to give birth furthermore to the third Principle,
wherein the spirit of the two principles might rest
and manifest itself in similitude.

27. And though each principle has its centre, the

first principle stands in magical quality, and its centre is fire, which cannot subsist without substance; therefore its hunger and desire is after substance.

28. And in regard to the first principle, if we speak only of one (though it is not single and solitary), we are to understand that the unfathomable will in the centre of the unground, in which the eternal Word is continually generated from eternity, is desirous; for the will desires the centre, viz. the word or heart.

29. Secondly, it desires that the heart should be manifest. For in the unground there is no manifestation, but an eternal nothingness; a stillness without being or colours, neither any virtue—(but in Desire colours, power and virtue come to be)—and is thus hidden in itself, and were eternally not manifest; for there would be no light, splendour or majesty, but a threefold spirit in itself, which were without source (*Qual*) of any being.

30. And thus we are to understand the essence of the deepest Deity, without and beyond Nature.

31. Further, we are to understand that the eternal will of the Deity desires to manifest itself from its own ground in the light of Majesty, whereby we apprehend the first will of the Father to the Son and to the light of Majesty to be desirous. And that in two ways : The first way to the centre of the Word; the second to Light or manifestation of the Word. And we find that every desire is attrahent, though in the unground there is nothing that can be drawn; hence the desire draws itself, and impregnates the other will of the Father,

which imaginates for the light of Majesty from the centre of his word or heart.

32. Now is the heart pregnant with Light, and the first will pregnant with Nature; and yet were none of this manifest, if the principle were not generated.

33. The Father generates from the first will the first Principle, as the nature which in fire attains to the highest perfection; and then he generates the second Principle in and from the other will to the Word, in that he desires the manifestation of the Word in the light of Majesty. Thus the fire of the second principle in the light of Majesty is a satisfying or appeasing of the first will : namely gentleness, which is opposed to the fire of the first principle, and quenches its fierce wrath, and brings it into an essential substance as into an eternal life. But the fire is hidden in the light, and gives to the light its power, strength and might, so that together there is an eternal union, and one without the other would not be.

Of the first Principle in itself ; what it is
(singly) in itself.

34. We are to consider Desire ; for every desire attracts what is in the desiring will.

35. God, however, desires only light, viz. the lustre from his heart, that he may shine forth in wisdom, and the whole God thus be manifest in himself, and by the forth-going Spirit out of himself, in the virgin of his wisdom; and that there be an eternal perfect joy, delight and satisfaction in him.

36. Now this can be accomplished in no other way than through fire, where the will is brought into the deepest sharpness of omnipotence, as it becomes consuming in fire. Contrariwise, light is a gentleness of the genetrix of the omni-substantiality.

37. But fire must have a genetrix to its origin and life, and here it appears in two lives and sources. And they are rightly called two principles, although there is only one ; but it is a twofold source in one being, and is in respect of the source regarded as two beings, as is to be seen in fire and light.

38. We now consider Desire, and find that it is a stern attraction, like an ʾeternal elevation or motion. For it draws itself into itself, and makes itself pregnant, so that from the thin freedom where there is nothing a darkness is produced. For the desiring will becomes by the drawing-in thick and full, although there is nothing but darkness.

39. The first will would now be free from the darkness, for it desires light, and yet cannot thus attain it. For the greater the desire is for freedom, the greater becomes the attraction and the sting of the essences, which take their rise in the drawing or desire.

40. Thus the will draws the more strongly into itself, and its pregnancy becomes the greater, and yet the darkness cannot comprehend the centre of the word or heart of the ternary ; for this centre is a degree deeper in itself, and yet is a band.

41. But the first will, in which the gestation of Nature takes place, is deeper still than the centre of the word, for it arises from the eternal Unground or Nothing; and thus the centre of the heart is shut up in the midst, the first will of the Father labouring to the birth of fire.

42. Now, we are to understand that in the stern attraction a very unyielding substance and being is produced. And so then substance from eternity has its origin; for the drawing gives sting, and the drawn gives hardness, matter from nothing, a substance and essentiality. The sting of the drawing dwells now in this essentiality, pierces and breaks; and all this from the desiring will which draws.

43. And here we are to recognize two forms of Nature, viz. sour (astringent), that is, Desire, and then the sting, which makes in the desire a breaking and piercing, whence feeling arises, that is, bitter, and is the second form of Nature, a cause and origin of the essences in Nature.

44. Now the first will is not satisfied with this, nor set at rest, but is brought thereby into a very great anguish; for it desires freedom in light, and yet, however, there is no brightness in freedom. Then it falls into terrible anguish, and so uplifts the desire for freedom, that the anguish, as a dying or sinking down through death, introduces its will into freedom out of the breaking, piercing, and powerful attracting.

45. Here, then, we understand the will in two ways: One, which rises in fierceness to generation of the wrath-fire; the other, which imaginates after the centre of the word, and, passing out of the anguish, as through a dying, sinks into the free life; and thus brings with it a life out of the torment

of anguish into freedom, so that the eternal Unground is recognized as a life, and from the Nothing an eternal life springs.

46. Seeing then the first movement of the will rises to the birth of fire, we recognize it as the first nature, viz. the Father's nature in fierce wrath ; and the other entrance of the will into freedom, into the centre of the heart, we recognize as the Divine Nature, as the life in light, in the power of the Deity.

47. It is now clear what the first will to fire operates and effects, viz. stern, hard, bitter, and great anguish, which is the third form of Nature ; for anguish is as the centre where life and will eternally take their rise. For the will would be free from the great anguish, and yet cannot. It would flee, and yet is held by the sourness (astringency) ; and the greater the will for flight becomes, the greater becomes the bitter sting of the essences and plurality.

48. It being unable then to flee or ascend, it turns as a wheel. And here the essences become mixed, and the plurality of essences enters into a mixed will, which is rightly called the eternal mind, where plurality in numberless essences is comprised in a mind, where always from an essence a will again may arise according to the property of that essence, whence the eternal wonders spring.

49. Seeing then the great and strong mind of the form of anguish goes thus in itself as a wheel, and continually breaks the stern attraction, and by the sting brings into plurality of essences ; but in anguish, in the wheel disposes again into a one, as

into a mind : therefore now the anguishful life is
born, viz. Nature, where there is a moving, driving,
fleeing and holding, as also a feeling, tasting and
hearing. And yet it is not a right life, but only
a Nature-life without a principle. For it has no
growth, but is like a frenzy or madness, where
something goes whirling in itself as a wheel, where
indeed there is a bond of life, but without understanding or knowledge ; for it knows not itself.

50. Further, we are to inquire concerning the
other will of the eternal Father which is called
God, which in the centre of its heart desires light
and the manifestation of the triad in wisdom. This
will is set or directed towards the *centrum naturae*,
for through Nature must the splendour of Majesty
arise.

51. Now, this other will in the Word of life has
freedom in itself ; and the anguishful will in the
sharpness of Nature desires freedom, that freedom
might be revealed in the anguish of the fierce
wrathful mind.

52. Whence then also anguish arises, that the
first will wishes to be free from the dark sourness
(astringency), and freedom desires manifestation ;
for it cannot find itself in itself without sharpness
or pain. For the will of freedom, which is called
Father, desires to manifest itself, and that it cannot
do without properties.

53. It is therefore desirous of properties, which
take their rise in anguish, in essences, in fire, thereby
to manifest its wonders, power and colours, which
without Nature cannot be.

54. Thus, the first will (which is called Father,

and is itself freedom) desires Nature, and Nature with great longing desires freedom, that it may be released from the torment of anguish. And it receives freedom in its sharp fierceness in the imagination, at which it is terrified as a flash ; for it is a terror of joy that it is released from the torment of anguish.

55. And in the terror arise two beings, a mortal one and a living one, to be understood thus :

56. The will which is called Father, which has freedom in itself, so generates itself in Nature, that it is susceptible of Nature, and that it is the universal power of Nature.

57. The terror of its Nature is a kindler of fire. For when the dark anguish, as the very fervent, stern being, receives freedom in itself, it is transformed in the terror, in freedom, into a flash, and the flash embraces freedom or gentleness. Then the sting of death is broken ; and there rises in Nature the other will of the Father, which he drew prior to Nature in the mirror of wisdom, viz. his heart of love, the desire of love, the kingdom of joy.

58. For in the Father's will fire is thus generated, to which the other will gives the power of gentleness and love. The fire takes the love-quality into its essence, and that is now its food, so that it burns, and gives from the consumption, from the terror, the joyous spirit.

59. That is, here, the Holy Spirit, who originally prior to Nature is the Father's Will-spirit, becomes manifest, and receives here the power of wonders; and proceeds thus from the Father (viz. from the first will to Nature), from the other will in Nature,

from fire, or from the terror of joy in the source of love, into the substantiality of gentleness.

60. For gentleness is also become desirous of the fire's property, and the desire draws the gentleness of the kingdom of joy into itself. That is now the water of eternal life, which the fire drinks, and gives therefrom the light of Majesty.

61. And in the light dwells the will of the Father and of the Son, and the Holy Spirit is the life therein. He reveals now the power of the gentle essentiality in the light, and that is colours, wonders and virtues.

62. And this is called virgin Wisdom; for it is not a genetrix, neither itself reveals anything, but the Holy Spirit is the revealer of its wonders. It is his vesture and fair adornment, and has in it the wonders, colours and virtues of the divine world; it is the house of the Holy Trinity, and the ornament of the divine and angelic world.

63. In its colours and virtues the Holy Spirit has revealed the choirs of angels, as well as all the marvels of created things, all which have been beheld from eternity in wisdom; without being indeed, but in wisdom as in the mirror, according to their figures; which figures have in the motion of the Father advanced into essence and into a creaturely existence, all according to the wonders of wisdom.

64. Now, understand us also concerning the other being, where in the terror Nature divides into two beings, as mentioned above: viz. one through the Father's will into fire or into the fire-world; and one through the Father's other will that is drawn

or generated in himself, into the majestic light-world.

65. And the other being, viz. the house of terror in itself, in death, in the darkness of the hostile source (*Qual*), which must stand thus in order that there may be an eternal longing in this anguish to be freed from the source. For this longing makes the first will to Nature eternally desirous to come to the aid of its being. Whence then in the Father's will mercy arises, which enters with freedom into the anguish, but cannot remain in the anguish, but goes forth in fire into the source of love.

66. That is, his other will, or his heart, issues in him as a fountain of love and mercy, from whence compassion has its origin, so that there is a pity on distress and misery, and a sympathy; viz. here, the Father's will, which is free, reveals itself in the fierceness of Nature, so that the fierce wrathfulness is mitigated.

67. But nevertheless on one part the terrible wheel of fierceness continues independently. For in the terror a mortification is brought about, not indeed a still death, but a mortal life; and resembles the worst thing, as is an aqua fortis or a poison in itself. For such a thing must be, if the *centrum naturae* is to subsist eternally.

68. And on the other part life proceeds out of death, and death must therefore be a cause of life. Else, if there were no such poisonous, fierce, fervent source, fire could not be generated, and there could be no essence nor fiery sharpness; hence also there would be no light, and also no finding of life.

69. The first will, which is called Father, finds itself thus in wonders ; and the other will, which is called Son, finds itself thus in power. Moreover, thus also the kingdom of joy arises ; for if there were no pain, there were also no joy. But this is the kingdom of joy, that life is delivered from anguish, although life has its origin thus.

70. And therefore the creatures have poison, viz. a gall, for their life. The gall is the cause that there is a mobility by which life rises ; for it occasions fire in the heart, and the right life is fire, but it is not the figure of life.

71. From the fire-life springs the right spirit, which goes forth from fire in the light ; it is free from fire as air, which nevertheless arises from fire, is free from fire.

72. For the right spirit, or in man the spirit which is generated from the soul's fire, has its property in the Light of life, which burns from fire. For it arises from death, it proceeds out of death, the hostile source has remained away from it in fire, and below fire, in the cause of fire, viz. in fierce wrathful death.

73. Fierce wrathful death is thus a root of life. And here, ye men, consider your death and also Christ's death, who has begotten us again out of death through the fire of God ; for out of death is the free life born. Whatever can go out from death is released from death and the source of wrath. That is now its kingdom of joy, that there is no longer any fierce source in it ; it has remained away from it in death (in the dark world). And thus out of death life attains eternal freedom,

where there is no more any fear or terror; for in life the terror is broken.

74. The right life is a power of joy, a perpetual well-being and pleasing delight; for there is no pain in it, save only a desire, which has all the property of pain, and yet the pain cannot uplift itself in it so as to kindle its property therein, for light and freedom hinder that.

CHAPTER II

Of the proprium of the principle. What the principle is, or what they all three are.

1. When life and movement appears, which previously existed not, a principle is present. Fire is a principle with its property, and light is also a principle with its property, for it is generated from fire, and yet is not the fire's property. It has also its own life in itself, but fire is cause thereof, and the terrible anguish is a cause of both.

2. But the will to anguish, which gives birth to the anguishful nature, and which is called Father, that it is impossible to search out. We inquire only how it brings itself into the highest perfection, into the being of the Holy Trinity; and how it manifests itself in three principles, and how the essence of each source arises; what essence is, whence life with the senses has its origin, and the wonder of all beings.

3. Thus, we recognize the third principle, or the source of this world, with the stars and elements, to be a creation from the marvels of the eternal wisdom.

4. The third principle manifests the first two, though each is manifest in itself. But the eternal Being has willed in his wonders, which have been beheld in wisdom, to manifest himself in such a property, viz. according to the ground of eternity,

according to the source of wrath and of love; and
has created all into a creaturely and figurative
being, evil and good according to the eternal origin.
As we plainly see that in this world there is evil and
good; of which, however, the devils are a great
cause, who in their creation have at the fall moved
more vehemently the fierce matrix in the wrath,
God having moved himself more exceedingly
according to the property of wrath, to cast them
forth out of light into the death of fierce wrathfulness; whereby also the heavenly Essence was
moved, so that very much which stood in freedom
has become shut up in the earthly essence.

5. As we see in gold and its tincture, which is
free from the earthly essence. For it resists fire
and every quality, no quality can hold it in check,
but only God's will; and that must come to pass
repeatedly by reason of the unworthiness of the
world.

6. And if we rightly consider the creation of this
world and the spirit of the third principle, viz. the
spirit of the great world with the stars and elements,
we find therein the property of the eternal world
as it were mixed, like unto a great marvel, whereby
God, the highest good, has willed to manifest and
bring into being the eternal wonders which existed
in mystery.

7. We find good and evil, and we find in all
things the *centrum naturae*, or the torture-chamber.
But we find especially the spirit of the great
world in two sources, viz. in heat and cold.
Here, by cold we understand the centre of the
sour sharp fierceness, and by heat the principle

of fire, and yet they have but one origin from one another.

8. Fire arises from the fierceness of the cold, and cold from the *centrum naturae*, viz. from the sour sharp anguish, where the sourness (astringency) contracts so strongly into itself and makes substance. As we are to know that in the motion of the Father at creation it has made earth and stones, although there was no matter for this, but only His own being, which is generated in two principles, viz. in the light-world and world of death, in two desires.

9. That which the fierceness attained in the motion became shaped into the terrestrial globe. And we find therein a diversity of things, evil and good; and it often happens that from the worst may be made the best, because the *centrum naturae* is therein. If it be brought into fire, the pure child of the eternal Essence may be extracted from it; when it is liberated from death, as is to be seen in gold.

10. In this world, however, we cannot attain the eternal fire, and therefore also can develop nothing from this principle. That is want of the eternal fire, which we do not reach but in imagination only, by which a man has power to lead life out of death and bring it into the divine substantiality. This can be done only in man; but what is outside of man belongs to God, and remains unto the renovation, to the end of this time.

11. And thus we give you to understand the nature and property of the principles. The first Principle lies in the fire of the will, and is a cause

of the two others, also of life and understanding ; and is an upholding of Nature, as well as of all the properties of the Father.

12. The second Principle lies in light, as in the fire of desire. This desire makes substance from the property of the first principle.

13. The first and second principle are Father and Son in eternity. One dwells in the other, and yet each retains its property. There is no mixing in the essence ; but one receives the other in desire, and the light dwells in the fire's desire, so that the fire's property gives its desire to the light, and the light to the fire.

14. Thus there is one being and not two, but two properties, whereof one is not the other, nor eternally can become so. As the spirit's property cannot be fire and light, and yet proceeds from fire out of light, and could not subsist either from fire or from light alone. Fire alone could not give it, neither could light, but the two give it. It is the life of both, and is one being only, but three properties, whereof one is not the other, as is to be seen in fire, light and air.

15. The third Principle has just these properties. It has also fire, light and spirit, that is, air ; and is in all particulars like to the eternal Being. But it has a beginning, and proceeds from the Eternal ; it is a manifestation of the Eternal, an awakening, image and similitude of the Eternal. It is not the Eternal ; but an essence has arisen in the eternal Desire, which has manifested itself therein and brought itself into a being like the Eternal.

16. Reason says : God has made this world out

of nothing. Answer: There was certainly for that no substance or matter that were outwardly palpable; but there was such a form in the eternal power in the will.

17. The creation of this world was brought about by an awakening of the Will-spirit. The inner will, which exists within in itself, has stirred up its own nature, as the centre, which, passing out of itself, is desirous of the light which is pressing forth from the centre. Thus the centre has seized out of itself a being in desire; that is, it has seized or made for itself being in its own imagination in desire, and has also laid hold of the light's nature.

18. It has with the beginning laid hold of the Eternal; and therefore the beings of this world must enter by figure again into the Eternal, for they have been apprehended in the Eternal. But whatever was made or seized from the beginning in desire, that returns into its aether as into the nothing, merely into the mirror of imagination again. That is not of the Eternal, but is and belongs to the eternal Magic in desire. Like as a fire swallows up and consumes a substance whereof nothing remains, but becomes again as it was when as yet it was no substance.

19. And thus we give you to understand what this world's existence is. Nothing else than a coagulated smoke from the eternal aether, which thus has a fulfilment like the Eternal. It shuts itself in a *centrum* of a substance, and finally consumes itself again; and returns again into the eternal Magic, and is but for a while a wonder as a

revelation of the Eternal, whereby the Eternal, which is manifest in itself, manifests itself also out of itself, and pours out its imagination ; and thus renews that which was seized or made by the motion in desire, that the end may again enter into the beginning.

20. For nothing can enter into the freedom of the Eternal, except it be like the Eternal, subsist in the fire of the will, and be as subtle as the light's substantiality, that is, as a water which can dwell in a being wherein the light can dwell, and convey its lustre through. This is not laid hold of by the *centrum naturae*, and though it be the property of Nature, yet it is something eternal.

21. Thus we give you to understand that all that is born in this world, which has substance, which proceeds not from the eternal Essence, inherits not the Eternal ; but its figure persists magically in the eternal Mystery, for it went originally at creation out of the Eternal. But its body and the entire substance of the source passes away, as a smoke is consumed ; for it is from the beginning, and goeth into the end.

22. But whatever arises from the eternal Essence, from the essentiality of the eternal Light, cannot pass away. That only in it perishes, which, proceeding from the temporal, has entered into the Eternal ; as the outer flesh, which through imagination was in man introduced into the Eternal ; that must be consumed like smoke.

23. But whatever originating from the eternal Imagination is re-introduced into the Eternal, persists eternally ; and that which is born from the

Eternal (understand, from the Eternal Nature), and
is in man the soul, remains eternally, for it has
arisen from the Eternal.

24. But if something be born from the eternal
centre of wrath, that may enter into its renovation, if it will.   As the Eternal Nature of the
essence of external Nature renews itself, and abandons that which it made in the beginning, and
retains only the magical image which it brought
out of the eternal will into the outward by the
Verbum Fiat at creation ; so may man also renew
that which he makes.   If he abandon the earthly,
then he may renew that which he has progenerated
from the Eternal ; but if it be not renewed, it
remains in the source.

25. For all that becomes not or is not as fire,
light and water, cannot subsist in freedom, but
remains in the source of that which it has awakened
or made in itself,—understand, from the *centrum
naturae*.   Whatever it has introduced into the
will of freedom will thus be for it a torment and
gnawing, or contrary opposite will, which it has
generated from its own nature, by which it has
made freedom dark for itself, so that the light
cannot shine through.   That will be its darkness.

26. For where the will is dark, there also the being
of the will, or its body, is dark ; and where the will
is in torment, there also the body is in torment.
For which cause the children of the light of freedom will be separated in the source of anguish from
the children of darkness, each into its principle.

27. Further, we give you to understand that each
principle generates its own life according to its

property. But fire is the bound of separation which satisfies the two eternal principles, darkness and light. To the darkness it gives its sting and the pang, and to the light its sensibility and life.

28. So also the third Principle has two properties, viz. heat and cold. Heat is the principle, and gives its sting and pang to the cold; and to the light it gives life and sensibility. The light in its turn gives its substantiality to the fire, so that it is united amicably with it. The cold gives also its property and substantiality to the fire, and the fire breaks this, and makes from its substantiality death and a dying. There is always, therefore, an enmity between heat and cold, and they are never at one.

29. But this they attain in their enmity, that life buds through death; for from heat and cold arises the growth of the third principle (in which we live outwardly). From cold there comes fruit out of the earth, as well as the body of all creatures, and, in the elements, substance. From heat there comes in its contention life into the body of all creatures and plants; as also in the deep of the elements it gives the spirit of the great world in diversity of figures. That is to say, where cold makes substance, there heat makes a spirit.

30. Thus is the Essence all in wrestling combat, that the wonders of the eternal world may become manifest in fragility, and that the eternal exemplar in the wisdom of God may be brought into figures. And that these models in the eternal Magic, in Mystery, may stand eternally to God's glory, and for the joy of angels and men; not indeed in

being, but in Mystery, in Magic, as a shadow of being, that it may be eternally known what God has wrought, and what he can and is able to do.

31. For, after the dissolution of this world, there remains in existence only what is eternal, as eternal spirits with the eternal substantiality of their bodies, together with the wonders wrought here, which stand in figure magically, by which the spirits will recognize the might and marvels of God.

32. We are now to consider the principles with their wonders. These are all three none else than the one God in his wonderful works, who has manifested himself by this world according to the property of his nature. And we are thus to understand a threefold Being, or three worlds in one another.

33. The first is the fire-world, which takes its rise from the *centrum naturae*, and Nature from the desiring will, which in eternal freedom has its origin in the unground, whereof we have not nor support any knowledge.

34. And the second is the light-world, which dwells in freedom in the unground, out of Nature, but proceeds from the fire-world. It receives its life and sensibility from fire. It dwells in fire, and the fire apprehends it not. And this is the middle world.

35. Fire in the *centrum naturae* before its enkindling gives the dark world; but is in its enkindling in itself the world of light, when it separates into light and leaves the centre in darkness, for it is only a source in itself, and a cause of life.

36. It has creatures, but they are of the same

fierce essence. They feel no pain; to them the light were a pain. But to the fallen devils, who in the principle were created in the world of light, to them the darkness is a pain, and fire a strength or might, for it is their right life, although according to many properties, by virtue of the *centrum naturae*, in accordance with that essence.

37. The third world is the outer, in which we dwell by the outer body with the external works and beings. It was created from the dark world and also from the light-world, and therefore it is evil and good, terrible and lovely. Of this property Adam was not to eat, nor imaginate thereinto; but the three worlds were to stand in him in order, that one might not comprehend the other, as in God himself. For Adam was created from all the three worlds, an entire image and similitude of God.

38. But seeing he has eaten of evil and good, and introduced the outer into the middle, the outer must now break off from the middle; and a separation takes place, in which the outer must return into its aether, and the middle remains.

39. Thus, if one see a right man, he may say: I see here three worlds standing, but not moving. For the outer world moves by the outer body, but the outer body has no power to move the light-world; it has only introduced itself into the world of light, whereby the light-world is become extinguished in man. He has, however, remained to be the dark world in himself; and the light-world stands in him immoveable, it is in him as it were hidden.

40. But if he be a right man by the new birth,

then it stands in him as light shines through water, and makes the essence mobile and desireful, so that the essence buds. Thus it is with the new man in the Light. And as we cannot move the light of the sun, so neither can we move the eternal Light or the light-world. It stands still and shines through everything that is susceptible of it, whatsoever is thin like a nothing, as indeed fire and water are; though all is substantial, but in reference to the external as a nothing.

41. Thus each principle has its growth from itself; and that must be, else all were a nothing.

42. The principle of fire is the root, and it grows in its root. It has in its proprium sour, bitter, fierceness and anguish; and these grow in its proprium in poison and death into the anguishful stern life, which in itself gives darkness, owing to the drawing-in of the harshness. Its properties make sulphur, mercury and salt; though the fire's property makes not Sul in sulphur, but the will of freedom makes Sul in Phur, whilst the principle goes forward.

43. But what advances into its properties is only Phur, viz. sternness, with the other forms in the centre. This is the chief cause of life and of the being of all things. Though it is bad in itself, yet it is the most useful of all to life and the manifestation of life. For there could be no life without this property, and this principle is grounded in the internal and external world; in the internal as imperceptible, in the external perceptible by its fierceness.

44. The second Principle has also its growth from

itself, for fire streams forth in light with its properties. But the Light transforms the fierce wrathful properties into a desire of love and joy. And therefore the fire's essence and property is wholly transformed in the Light, so that out of anguish and pain comes a love-desire, out of the stinging and raging a friendly sensible understanding.

45. For the Light kindles the essences with the quality of love, so that they give from themselves a growth in the property of the spirit : viz. a friendly will, morality, virtue, piety, patience in suffering, hope to be delivered from evil; continually speaking of God's wonderful works in desire and joy, ringing forth, singing and rejoicing in the works and wonders of God; always desiring to do right, to hinder evil and wickedness; always wishing to draw one's neighbour by love into the world of light; fleeing from evil; always subduing the evil affections with patience, in hope of being released therefrom; rejoicing in the hope of that which the eyes see not and external Reason knows not; continually pressing forth out of evil, and introducing the desire into the divine Being; always wishing to eat of God's bread.

46. These properties hath the new man who is born again from the light-world. These are his fruits, which the light-world continually brings forth in him quite hiddenly to the old Adam, and continually mortifies the old Adam of this world, and is always in combat with him. Which old Adam must therefore follow the new man; in sooth like a lazy ass which is obliged to carry the sack, his master continually lashing him on. Thus doth the

new man to the old ; he compels him, so that he must do what he would fain not do. What pertains to the joy of this world were more acceptable to the old ass ; but he must thus be the servant.

47. Secondly, the principle has its growth, and gives its fruit to the third principle generally, viz. to the spirit of the great world, so that the external and internal *turba* are held in check. It presses through and gives fruitfulness ; it stays the fierceness of the stars, and breaks the constellation of the spirits and also of the firmamental heaven. It resists the wrath of the devil and the devices of wicked men, so far however as there are found saints who are worthy of it.

48. The third Principle has also its growth ; and therein were generated and created from what is inward the stars and elements, which in this place together with the sun are called the third principle. For the two inward worlds, viz. the fire-world and light-world, have manifested themselves by the third principle ; and all is mixed together, good and evil, love and enmity, life and death. In every life there is death and fire ; also, contrariwise, a desire of love, all according to the property of the internal world. And two kinds of fruit grow therefrom, evil and good; and each fruit has both properties. They show themselves moreover in every life in this world, so that wrath and the evil quality are always fighting against love, each property seeking and bearing fruit. What the good makes, that the evil destroys ; and what the evil makes, that the good destroys. It is a perpetual war and contention, for the properties of both the inward

principles are active externally; each bears and produces fruit to the internal kingdom, each will be lord.

49. Cold, as the issue from the inward centre, from the fierceness of death, will be lord, and be continually shutting up in death; it always awakens the sting of death. And heat, as the issue from the right fire, will also be lord; it would subdue and consume all, and will be always crude or unfashioned, without a body. It is a spirit, and desires only a spirit-life. It gives sting to the cold, for oftentimes it kills it, so that it must forego its right and surrender itself to the heat.

50. In the same way the sun, or the light, will also have reason and be lord. It overcomes heat and cold, for it makes in its lucid gentleness water, and introduces in the light's spirit a friendly spirit, viz. the air; although fire gives the force of the wind, and the sun the gentle spirit which is properly called air. It is indeed one, but has two properties, one according to the fire, as a terrible uplifting, and one according to the light, as a gentle life.

51. The external principle is thus a perpetual war and contention, a building and breaking; what the sun or the light builds, that the cold destroys, and the fire consumes it entirely.

52. In this struggle its growth rises in mere combat and disunion; the one draws out of the earth its fruitfulness, the other destroys or swallows it up again.

53. In all animals it causes malice and strife; for all animals and all the life of this world, except man, is only a fruit of the third principle and

possesses only the life of the third principle, both
its spirit and body are only this. And all that
moves in this world, and man by his spirit and
visible body in flesh and blood, is also only the fruit
of this same essence, and nothing else at all.

54. But seeing he has in himself also the two
inward worlds (which give him the right understanding, discernment and disposition ; which also
during this time of the earthly and elemental body
are in conflict with one another), let him therefore
take heed ; the world that he makes lord in him,
the same will eternally be lord in him. During
this time he can break, and no farther. When
the outward breaks, then all stands in its aether.
The soul is free, and is the *punctum*, and has the
understanding ; it may incline whither it will, and
may support which principle it pleases; the aether
into which it enters, there it is eternally.

55. And thus we understand the foundation of
the three principles (like as the tongue of the beam
of a balance) ; what God and eternity is and is able
to do, and what growth each principle gives from
itself, from its property, and how we are to investi-
gate the ground of Nature.

Thus the first part or point is completed.

THE SECOND POINT

CHAPTER III

1. In God's kingdom, viz. in the light-world, no more than one principle is truly known. For the Light rules, and the other sources and properties all exist hiddenly as a mystery; for they must all serve the Light, and give their will to the Light. And therefore the wrath-essence is transformed in the Light into a desire of light and of love, into gentleness.

2. Although the properties, viz. sour, bitter, anguish and the sharp pang in fire remain eternally, even in the light-world, yet none of them is manifest in its property; but they are all of them together only causes of life, mobility and joy.

3. That which in the dark world is a pang, is in the light-world a pleasing delight; and what in the dark is a stinging and enmity, is in the light an uplifting joy. And that which in the dark is a fear, terror and trembling, is in the light a shout of joy, a ringing forth and singing. And that could not be, if originally there were no such fervent, austere source.

4. The dark world is therefore the ground and origin of the light-world ; and the terrible evil must be a cause of the good, and all is God's.

5. But the light-world is only called God ; and the principle between the light-world and dark world is called God's anger and fierce wrath. If this be awakened, as by the devil and all wicked men, these are then abandoned of the Light and fall into the dark world.

6. The dark world is called death and hell, the abyss, a sting of death, despair, self-enmity and sorrowfulness ; a life of malice and falsehood, in which the truth and the light is not seen and is not known. Therein dwell the devils and the damned souls ; also the hellish worms, which the *Fiat* of death has figured in the motion of the omnipresent Lord.

7. For hell hath in the darkness the greatest constellation of the fervent, austere power. With them all is audible as a loud noise. What rings in the Light, knocks and thumps in the Dark, as is to be seen in the thing men use to strike upon, that it gives a ringing sound. For the sound is not the thing ; as a bell that is rung is itself not a sound, but only a hardness and a cause of the sound. The bell receives the stroke as a knocking, and from the hard knocking proceeds the ringing sound. The reason is this, that in the matter of the bell there is an element, which, at creation, in the motion of the omnipresent God, was shut up in the hardness ; as is to be seen in the metalline tincture, if men would not be so mad and blind.

8. We recognize, then, that in hell, in the abyss,

there are many and divers spirits, not only devils, but many hellish worms according to the property of their constellation, and void of understanding. As in this world there are irrational animals—worms, toads and serpents—so has also the abyss such in the fierce wrathful world. For all willed to be creaturely, and is gone into a being, so that the wrath-mirror also exhibited its wonders and manifested itself.

9. There is indeed no feeling of pain in the hellish worms, for they are of the same essence and property. It is their life, and is a nature that is hidden to the outer world ; but the Spirit of God who in all three principles is himself the source in accordance with each property, he knows it and reveals it to whom he will.

10. If now we would say how the three principles are united together, we must place fire in the middle as the highest force, which brings to each principle a satisfying life and a spirit that it requires. There is, therefore, in the principles no strife ; for fire is the life of all the principles,—understand, the cause of life, not the life itself. To the abyss it gives its pang, viz. the sting, so that death finds itself in a life ; else the abyss were a stillness. It gives it its fierceness, which is the life, mobility and original condition of the abyss ; else there were a still eternity and a nothing.

11. And to the light-world fire gives also its essence, else there were no feeling nor light therein, and all were only one. And yet beyond fire a Nothing, as an eye of wonders that knew not itself, in which were no understanding ; but an

eternal hiddenness, where no seeking or doing were possible.

12. And to the third principle, viz. to the kingdom of this world, fire gives also its essence and quality, whereby all life and growth rises. All sense, and whatever is to come to anything, must have fire. There springs nothing out of the earth without the essence of fire. It is a cause of all the three principles, and of all that can be named.

13. Thus fire makes a union of all the three principles, and is for each the cause of being. One principle fights not against another, but the essence of each desires only its own, and is always in combat; and if that were not, then all were a still nothingness. Each principle gives to the other its power and form, and there is a perpetual peace between them.

14. The dark world has the great pain and anguish which gives birth to fire, so that the will longs after freedom, and freedom longs after manifestation, viz. after essences, and gives itself to fierceness that it may thus manifest itself. And it is brought thus into fire, so that from fierceness and freedom a fire arises. It gives itself to fierceness to swallow up in death; but passes out of death with the received essences into a sphere of its own, as into a special world or source; and dwells in itself unapprehended by death and the dark world, and is a light in itself.

15. Thus are death and fierceness a mother of fire, also a cause of the light-world; a cause, moreover, of all the essence of the third principle, a cause of all the essences in all lives. How then

should one principle fight against another, if each vehemently desires the other?

16. For the angelic light-world, and also this our visible world, must have the essence of dark death for their life and source; there is a continual hunger after it.

17. But each principle makes the source according to its property. It gives to the evil its good, and unites itself with it, and of three makes one, so that there is no strife between the three principles. But in the essence there is strife; and that must be, or all were a nothing.

18. But we are to consider whence enmity has its origin. God has in each principle created creatures from the nature and proprium of the principle, therein to remain. And if they remain not therein, but introduce another thing by their imagination into themselves, into their property, that is an enmity and torment to them, as to the devil and fallen man. Both these are gone out from the light-world; the devil into the abyss of the strong wrath-power through pride, and man into this world, into the mystery of multiscience, as into the wonders.

19. And now man has a difficulty and struggle to come out again; and this world, into which he has entered, holds him, for it will have him; and if he go out from it by force, it becomes hostile to him, assails him, and will not suffer him in itself.

20. Hence it is that the children of this world do hate, vex, strike, kill and drive from them the children of light, for the spirit of this world impels them thereto. To which also the devil helps, for

he knows that this world rests upon the abyss, and that he will receive the children of this world at the dissolution of this Mystery into his kingdom. Therefore he drives the children of God from this world, lest they introduce his children of this world along with them into the world of light.

21. But if man had been created for this world, he would certainly let him alone ; but he continually desires to recapture his royal seat which he had, and from which he was cast out ; and if he may in no wise obtain it, he would deny it to the children who are to possess it.

22. Now this is for man highly to consider, and not to be so blind. Every man has entered into the mystery of this world ; but he should not therefore as a prisoner enter also into the earthly craving of the confining of death, but should be a discerner and knower of the Mystery, and not the devil's butt and fool. He should by the imagination continually go out again into the light-world for which he was created, in order that the light may give him lustre, that he may know himself and see the outer Mystery. Then he is a man. But if not, he is the devil's fool and the ape of the light-world. Just as an ape will be knowing and play with everything, and imitate everything, so it is with the earthly man, who is but an ape. His juggling tricks with the light-world, when he presses not thereinto with earnestness, but only plays therewith,—this the devil derides, and accounts him a fool. And so he is ; he is an animal-man. So long as he is attached with his will to the external, and regards this world's good

as his treasure, he is only a man with this world's essence, and not with the essence of God's light-world ; and he gives his body to this world or to the earth, and his soul to the abyss of the dark world.

23. Thus we give you to understand that in the tree of the three principles, these agree very well together, but not the creatures; for the creatures of each principle desire not the others. And there is a strong bar and closure between them, so that we know not, nor shall we see the others.

24. But the devil's envy wars against the human race, for they have possessed his seat. Therefore it is said : Man, seek thyself, and see what thou art, and beware of the devil. So much on the second point, how the three principles can agree unitedly together.

THE THIRD POINT

CHAPTER IV

1. A thing that is one, that has only one will, contends not against itself. But where there are many wills in a thing, they become contending, for each would go its own conceived way. But if one be lord of the other, and has entirely full power over all the others, so that it can break them if they obey it not; then the thing's multiplicity has its existence in one reality, for the multitude of wills all give themselves to obedience of their lord.

2. And thus we give you to understand life's contrariety, for life consists of many wills. Every essence may carry with it a will, and indeed does so. For sour, bitter, anguish and acid is a contrarious source, each having its own property, and wholly adverse one to the other. So is fire the enemy of all the others, for it puts each source into great anguish, so that there is a great opposition between them, the one being hostile to the other, as is to be seen in heat and cold, fire and water, life and death.

3. So likewise the life of man is at enmity with

itself. Each form is hostile to the other, and not only in man, but in all creatures; unless the forms of life obtain a gentle, gracious lord, under whose control they must be, who can break their might and will. That is found in the Light of life, which is lord of all the forms, and can subdue them all; they must all give their will to the Light. And they do it also gladly, for the Light gives them gentleness and power, so that their harsh, stern, bitter, anguishful forms are all transformed into loveliness. They all give their will to the Light of life, and the Light gives them gentleness.

4. Plurality is thus transformed into unity, into one will which is called the mind, and is the fountain from which the one will is able to draw evil and good. This is done by imagination, or by representation of a thing that is evil or good; and hence the thing's property is susceptible of the same property in the life. The life's property seizes the property of the thing represented, be it either a word or a work, and enkindles itself therewith in itself. It kindles also the other forms of life therewith, so that they begin to qualify, and every property burns in its source, either in love or wrath, all according to the nature represented. Whatever the imagination has seized, that it introduces into the mind.

5. We give you therefore to understand that when the mind thus enkindles itself in a form, it enkindles the whole spirit and body, and forthwith carries its imagination into the inmost fire of the soul, and awakens the inmost *centrum naturae*. This, when it is enkindled, be it in wrath or love,

apprehends itself in all the seven forms of Nature, which reach after the spirit of the soul's will, wherein is the noble image in which God reveals himself, and introduce their enkindled fire there-into. As you have a similitude of this in fire : According to the matter in which it burns, such a light does it give ; as is to be seen in sulphur compared with wood, and in many things besides.

6. We understand then by this, that whatever nature and property the fire hath, such a property getteth also the light and the power of the light.

7. Seeing then our noble image of God stands in the Light of life, in the soul's fire, it is highly recognizable by us how the spirit of the soul's will or the noble image is corrupted, and becomes enkindled in the source of wrath, often also in the source of love. And we see here our great danger and misery, and do rightly understand why Christ has taught us patience, love and meekness, viz. that the soul's fire kindle not itself in wrath, also that we give not occasion to others to kindle their souls' fire in wrath, in order that God's kingdom be not hindered.

8. Herein we recognize our heavy fall, that Adam has introduced into our souls' fire earthly matter, which burns as often as a source is awakened in the centre of the property of wrath. We see thus how we lie captive in God's wrath between anger and love, in great danger.

9. And we give you this highly to recognize. You know, as we have set forth above and in all our books, how from fire light proceeds as another principle, and yet has the fire's property and power,

for the fire's centre gives them to the light's centre. And how the light is also desirous, and has a matrix of longing desire, which makes itself pregnant in desire with the power of the light, viz. with the gentleness of the light; and in this pregnancy lies the substance of the light, that is, in the pure love of the Divine Nature.

10. And then we have informed you how the fire draws this substance into itself, uses it for its light's essence, and swallows it up in itself, but gives from the essence another spirit, which is not fire. As indeed you see that fire gives two spirits: One that is furious and consuming, consisting of fierceness as property of the first matter; and secondly, an air-spirit, which is the property of the light's gentleness.

11. We are now to consider in what matter fire burns in the first essence. In whatever it has kindled itself, in love or anger, that is, in earthly or divine desire, such a fire it is, and gives also such a fire of light, and such a spirit from the fire of light.

12. Now, if the matter of the first fire, wherein the fire burns, be good, then has the other fire of light also a good property, savour and source, and gives also a good, powerful, lovely light, and from the light's centre also a good and powerful spirit; and this spirit is the similitude of God, the noble image.

13. But if the first fire be evil in its essence, and has an evil matter in which it burns, then is also the life's light a false source and a dim shining, as is to be seen in a sulphurous light; and the centre

of this desiring light brings also out of its property such a matter into its fire, and the fire gives such a spirit from itself.

14. It is now evident what spirit can or cannot attain the freedom of God. For the soul's spirit or the image which has in itself the dim, dark property, cannot be capable of the clear light of God. Further, if it has in itself fierce wrathful essences and qualities, it cannot unite with the gentleness of God and inqualify with it; for wrath is enmity against love and gentleness, and love suffers not wrath within it. Here they are separated: love thrusts wrath from it, and neither does wrath desire any more the property of love.

15. For as soon as fire gives spirit from itself, it is perfect, and separates into its proprium, be it a spirit of light, or a dark wrathful sulphurous spirit. And into the same essence from which it is gone out does it desire to return again; for it is its property, be it in love or enmity to love.

16. Accordingly we understand what spirits or souls live in the source of enmity, and how enmity originally arises, so that a life is at enmity with itself from the first matter unto the life's light. The cause lies in the wheel of Nature, in the seven spirits or forms, each of which has its own property; and in whichever property the mind becomes enkindled, such a property getteth its soul's fire together with the will's spirit, which straightway aspires after substance and being, how it may realize that with which the spirit of the will is pregnant.

17. Now it is necessary to break the earthly

will's power and kill the old evil Adam, and bring his will-spirit by compulsion and force out of wickedness. For here, in this time, that is possible; because the third principle by the water which gives gentleness is attached to the centre of the inward nature, and holds it captive as it were in its quality.

18. But if the spirit of the soul's will, as the inward centre of light, breaks off from the outward and remains alone, then the soul's spirit remains in its property. For there is little remedy unless the spirit of the will have in the time of the external life turned round to God's love, and attained this as a sparkle in the inward centre. Then something may be done. But in what agony and travail that is done, experiences full well the sparkle of love, which has to break down dark fierce death. It is purgatory enough to it. In what enmity life stands, in terror and anguish, till it can sink into the sparkle, into the freedom of God, he indeed experiences who departs from this world so nakedly with little light. This, the present much too wise world regards as a jesting matter; but what kind of knowledge it has, it shows by its doing.

19. And thus we understand also the devil's fall, who was an angel; how he imagined back into the centre of the first property, and sought great strength and might (as the present world seeks great might and honour), and despised the light of love. Albeit he supposed the light would burn for him thus (and the world also hopes and supposes the light of God shall burn in its pomp),

and he willed to enkindle himself still more vehemently, to see if he could dominate over all thrones, and over the essence of the Deity in gentleness; which proved to be his fall, as will happen also to the present world.

20. Therefore let every man learn hereby to beware of pride and covetousness; for the devil's fall came through pride and covetousness, in that he kindled in himself the centre of the dark world. Hence he was cast out of the light-world into the dark world. And thus it fares with all men, who, abandoning meekness and humility, enter into wrath, pride, covetousness and envy. All these imaginate into the centre of the dark Nature, as into the origin of Nature, and withdraw into the dark fire of the source of anguish, where the noble image is introduced into another quality, so that it must be in fear and enmity, each form of life being hostile to the other.

21. And we see also very exactly herefrom, how God's kingdom is found only in the bright clear light in freedom, in love and gentleness; for that is the property of the white clear light. As is to be seen in outer nature, that where there is a pleasant, mild and sweet matter for the outer fire (which is but the fierceness of the inner fire), that also a pleasant light and odour arise from it. Much more is this so in the spirit-fire, to which no comprehensible or external being belongs; but where the seven spirits of Nature make in themselves a fire, which is only a property and a source of fire, as indeed the dark world and light-world stand in such a spiritual property.

22. As also the inner man, who is from the Eternal and who goeth into the Eternal; he has only the two worlds in him. The property to which he turns himself, into that world is he introduced, and of that world's property will he eternally be, and enjoy the same; either a source of love from the light-world of gentleness, or a hostile source from the dark world.

23. Here he buds and grows in the middle world between the light-world and dark world; he may give himself up to which he pleases. The essence which obtains the dominion in him, whether fierceness or gentleness, the same he embraces, and it hangs unto him and leads him; it gives him morals and will, and unites itself wholly with him; and thereinto man brings the spiritual man, viz. the image which God created from His being, from all the three principles.

24. Therefore it is said: Take the cross upon thee; enter into patience, into a meek life. Do not what the dark centre of wrath incites thee to, nor what the falsehood and pleasure of this world entice thee to; but break both their wills. Neither provoke any to anger. For if thou deal falsely, thou dost incense thy brother and hinder the kingdom of God.

25. Thou shouldst be a leader into the kingdom of God, and enkindle thy brother with thy love and meekness, that he may see in thee God's essence as in a mirror, and thus in thee take hold also with his imagination. Doest thou this, then bringest thou thy soul, thy work, likewise thy neighbour or brother into God's kingdom, and enlargest the

kingdom of heaven with its wonders. This has
Christ taught us, saying : If any smite thee on
one cheek, offer him the other also; if any take
away thy cloak, withhold not from him thy coat
also (Matt. v. 39, 40); that he may have in thee a
mirror and retreat into himself, see thy meekness,
acknowledge thou art God's child, and that God's
Spirit leads thee ; that he may learn of thee, descend into himself and seek himself. Else, if thou
oppose him with defiance and spite, his spite becomes
kindled still more, and at last he thinks he is acting
right to thee. But thus he must certainly recognize
he doth thee wrong.

26. And as God's love resists all wicked men,
and the conscience often dissuades from evil, so
also thy meekness and patience go to his bad conscience, and arraign the conscience in itself before
God's light in the wrath. In this way many a
wicked man goes out from his wickedness, descends
into himself and seeks himself. Then God's Spirit
puts him in mind of thy patience, and sets it before
his eyes, and so he is drawn thereby into repentance
and abstinence.

27. Not that one should not defend oneself
against a murderer or thief, who would murder
and steal. But where one sees that any is eager
upon unrighteousness, one should set his fault
openly with a good light before his eyes, and freely
and of good will offer him the Christian richly-
loving heart ; that he may find actually and in
fact, that it is done out of love-zeal to God, and
that love and God's will are more to that man than
the earthly nature, and that he purposely will not

consent to anything passionate or evil being done ;
that he may see that the children of God do love
more the love of God and do cleave more to it than
to any temporal good ; and that God's children
are not at home in this world, but only pilgrims,
who gladly relinquish everything of this world,
so that they may but inherit the kingdom of
heaven.

28. All this the Spirit of God puts before the
evil-doer in the life's light, and exhorts him thereby to conversion.   But if he will not, then the
wrath of God makes hellish fire from it, and finally
gnaws him, to see if even yet he would know himself and repent.   Persisteth he in wickedness, then
is he a wholly evil tree, grown in the wrath of God,
and belongs to the abyss, to the dark world of
anguish, to the dark God Lucifer ; there he must
devour his own abominations.   So much on the
third point.

THE FOURTH POINT

How the holy and good tree of eternal
life grows through and out of all the
growths of the three principles, and is
laid hold of by none.

CHAPTER V

1. A thing that dwells in itself can be grasped by
nothing, for it dwells in nothing; there is nothing
before it that can hold it in check, and it is free also
from the thing without it.

2. And thus we give you to understand concerning the divine power and light, which dwells in
itself and is comprehended in nothing; nothing
touches it, unless it be of the property thereof.
It is everywhere in Nature, yet Nature touches it
not (understand, the outer Nature of the world).
It shines therein as the sun in the elements. The
sun shines in water, also in fire and through the
air, and yet is not seized or held by any of them.
It gives to all beings power, and makes the essential
spirits lovely and joyous. It draws by its power
essence out of the earth, and not only essence, but
also the being of the essences, which gives out of
the essence a body.

3. What the sun does in the third principle by
transforming all hostile essence and quality into

gentleness, that God's light does in the forms of the Eternal Nature.

4. It shines in them and also from them; that is, it kindles the forms of Nature, so that they all obtain the Light's will, and unite themselves and give themselves up wholly to the Light; that is, they sink down from their own essence and become as if they had no might in themselves, and desire only the Light's power and might. The Light accordingly takes their power and might into itself, and shines from this same power. And thus all the forms of Nature attain to the Light, and the Light together with Nature is but one will, and the Light remains lord.

5. Else, if the wills in the stern forms of Nature will be lord, there is a separation and an eternal enmity. For one form is always at enmity with the other; each elevates itself. And therefrom comes contrariety, that a creature is so evil, wrathful and hostile, that often life is at strife in itself.

6. And as we know that the Light comes to the aid of the stern life of Nature, of the properties of the essences, so that a joyous life arises, and is thus changed in the Light; so also we know that the life of dark wrathfulness is the enemy of the Light, for it cannot catch the Light. The eternal Light shines through the darkness, and the darkness cannot comprehend it; for the plurality of wills in the dark Nature are all shut up in death; the Light shines not in them, but through them; they seize not, nor do they see the Light. Nevertheless, the Light is in the dark world, but it fills not the darkness; and therefore the essences of

the dark world remain a hostile poison and death, the essences being at enmity with themselves.

7. Thus there are three principles in one another, and one comprehends not the other; and the eternal Light cannot be laid hold of by anything, unless that thing fall into death, and give its essence voluntarily to the fire of Nature, and pass with its essential will out of itself into the Light, and abandon itself wholly to the Light; and desire to will or to do nothing, but commit its will to the Light, that the Light may be its will.

8. Thus the Light seizes it, and it also the Light. And thus the evil will is given up to the Light, and the Light gives its power to the malignity, and makes of the malignity a friendly good will, which is only a love-desire; for the gentleness of the Light has wholly embodied itself in the hostile will.

9. So then God's will is done, and the evil is transformed into good, and God's love shines from his anger and fierce wrath; and no wrath is known in God's Eternal Nature. Thus we are to understand how the eternal Light, or the eternal Power-tree, shines through all the three principles, unapprehended by any of them; for so long as an essence is out of God's will (viz. the gentle light-will), so long is it solitary and dwells in itself, and comprehends nothing of God. But if it unite itself to God, and break and sink its own will, then it is one spirit in and with God, and God shines from that essence.

10. And we understand also why the wicked soul, as well as the devil, sees not and knows not

God ; namely, because their will will not unite itself to God, it will itself be lord. It remains accordingly without God, only in itself, and God remains also in himself ; and so one dwells in the other, and knows nothing of the other, for one turns its back to the other, and sees not the face of the other.

11. And thus the world of light knows nothing of the devils, and the devils know nothing of the world of light, save only this, that they were once in it. They represent it to themselves as one who sees in imagination ; although the light-world no longer yields itself up to their imagination, neither do they imaginate after it, for it terrifies them ; also they are ashamed about it.

12. So likewise we are to understand concerning the outer world. God's light shines through and through, but is apprehended only by that which unites itself thereunto. Seeing then this outer world is as it were dumb and without understanding in respect of God, therefore it remains in its own will, and carries its own spirit in itself, although God has given it a Nature-god, viz. the sun, into which every being should cast its will and desire ; whatever is in this world and does not do so, that remains in itself a great malignity and is its own enmity.

13. And this world is recognized as a special principle because it has a Nature-god of its own, namely the sun ; and yet truly the light of the Deity shines through all, through and through. The light of the sun takes essence from God's fire, and God's fire from God's light. And thus the light of the sun gives this power to the elements, and

they give it to the creatures, also to the plants of the earth ; and all that is of a good property receives thus God's power as a lustre through the mirror of wisdom, from whence it has its growth and life.

14. For God is present to every being, but not every being receives him into its essence ; but as in the mirror of the aspect in the sun's virtue ; for the sun proceeds from the eighth number. Its root from which it receives its brightness is the eternal fire, but its body is in this world. Its desire is directed wholly into this world, in which it shines; but its first root is in the first world, in the fire of God. This world gives being to its desire, and it gives its power to being, and fills every being in this world, as God's light does the divine light-world. And if God's fire should burn no more, the sun would be extinguished, and also the divine light-world ; for God's fire gives essence to both, and is a principle of both. And if the dark world were not, neither would these two be ; for the dark world gives occasion for God's fire.

15. The three worlds must accordingly be in one another, for nothing can subsist without a ground. For the dark world is the ground of Nature ; and the eternal unfathomable will, which is called Father, is the ground of the dark world, as above set forth. And the light-world is hidden in the dark world, and also the dark world in the light-world.

16. It is to be understood thus : This world is shut up in the wrath of God as in death ; for wrath springs up in this world's essence. If that were not so, then might this world's essence seize God's light.

17. Thus this world receives only a reflection of God through the sun's power. The sun is not God's light, for it shines not wholly in divine essence, but shines in elemental essence. It has God's fire as its root, but is filled with this world's essence. For it is desirous as a magical craving, and receives in its imagination and craving the power of the stars and elements; and from this it shines also.

18. Though God's fire is its root, yet it belongs not to God's kingdom. And here we understand how the devil is the poorest creature ; for he cannot move a leaf except wrath be therein, and then he moves it according to the property of wrath. For the light and the power of this world is repugnant to him ; he enters not with his will into the property of the light, neither is he able to do so. He stands backward to the light of the sun in his figure and property, and therefore the sun's light profits him nothing. And all that grows in the sun's power, that unites itself to the sun, that he is enemy to ; his will enters not readily thereinto.

CHAPTER VI

1. If we consider all this, and pass from the inward world into this outward visible world, we find that the essence of the external world has proceeded from the internal, viz. from the imagination or desire of the internal world. And we shall find in the external world the property of the two inward worlds; also how the wills of both properties are moving and manifest in the external world. And then how the good, or the essence which has proceeded from the light-world, is shut up in wrath and death; and how the divine power activates all, so that all grows through and out of the fierceness of death.

2. For the earthly tincture has no communion or fellowship with the heavenly in the light-world. We find, however, in the earth another tincture which has fellowship with the heavenly, as in the precious metals, but is hidden in them.

3. And we understand thus the motion and the *Fiat* of the two eternal worlds, viz. the dark world and the light-world: Each has longed after being; and as God put himself in motion once for all, one world could not be moved without the other.

4. For the dark world contains the first centre of Nature, and the light-world the other centre, viz. the heart of God, or the Word of power of the Deity; and one world is not separated from the other.

5. Hereby we should recognize in what danger we stand, and think where we would plunge with our will. For if we plunge into the earthly craving, it captures us; and then the qualification of the abyss is our lord, and the sun our temporal god.

6. But if we plunge with our will into the world out of this world, then the light-world captures our will, and God becomes our lord; and we abandon the earthly life of this world, and take with us whatever has come from the light-world into us,— understand, into Adam; the same is carried out of this world with the will which becomes one spirit with God.

7. Reason says: Where are then the three worlds? It would have absolutely a separation, in which one were beyond or above the other. That, however, cannot possibly be, else the eternal un-fathomable Essence were bound to sever itself. But how can that sever itself which is a nothing, which has no place, which is itself all? That cannot enter into particular existence which has no ground, which cannot be comprehended, which dwells in itself and possesses itself; but it proceeds out of itself, and manifests itself out of itself.

8. It makes a thing out of itself, which in itself is but a will. In itself it is a spirit, but makes out of itself a form of spirit, and the form makes a being according to the property of the spirit. As indeed this world is a being, and the inward spirit possesses it. He is in every place, yet the place comprehends him not, but he comprehends the place. The place knows nothing of him, but it

feels him; for he is the power and the spirit in the place. His will goes through being, and being has no eyes to see him, but he is the seeing of the place; and is himself no place or position, but makes for himself an unfathomable position, where there is no measurement. He is all, and yet also like to a nothing in comparison with the external. What he gives out of himself, that he possesses too; he passes not into it, but he is there before being occupies the place. The place contains but a reflection of his will, as one sees one's form in a mirror, and yet cannot take hold upon it; or as the sunshine is not laid hold of in water, yet the water feels it and receives the lustre; or as the earth receives power from the sun, so that it brings forth fruit. In this way God dwells in all beings, and permeates and pervades all, yet is laid hold of by nothing.

9. And as we understand that the earth has a great hunger and desire after the sun's power and light, in which it draws to itself and becomes susceptible of the sun's power and light, which without desire could not be; in like manner outer nature hungers after the inner, for the outward form arises from the inner. Thus outer nature receives in itself the form of the inner as a lustre or power; for it cannot seize the inward spirit, inasmuch as he dwells not in the outer, but possesses himself in himself in the inner.

10. But outer nature receives by the mirror the form of the spirit, as water does the lustre of the sun. We are not to think that the inner is far from the outer, like the body of the sun is

from the water; though neither is that so, that the sun is far from the water, for the water has the sun's essence and property, else it would not catch the sun's lustre. Although the sun is a *corpus*, yet the sun is also in the water, but not manifest; the *corpus* makes the sun manifest in the water. And we are to know that the whole world would be nothing but sun, and the *locus* of the sun would be everywhere, if God was to kindle and manifest it; for every being in this world catches the sun's lustre. There is in all a mirror, that the power and form of the sun may be received in all that is animate and inanimate, in all the four elements and their essence and substance.

11. And so it is also with the inner light-world. It dwells in the outer world, and this receives power from it. It grows up in the outward power, and this knows nothing of it; it only feels the power, and the inward light it cannot behold; only in its life's mirror it receives the reflection thereof, for the inward power makes in the outward form a likeness of itself.

12. And thus then we are to recognize man. He is the inner and outer world (the cause, moreover, of the inner world in himself), and, so far as belongs to him, also the dark world. He is all three worlds; and if he remain standing in co-ordination, so that he introduce not one world into the other, then he is God's likeness.

13. He should introduce the form or the mirror of the light-world into the outer world, and also into the inmost dark world, and bring the power of the middle or light-world into the mirror, and

then he is susceptible of the divine light; for essence seizes not the light, but the power of the light. But the mirror of power catches the light, as water does the sun; for water is as a clear mirror in comparison with earth.

14. Now if water be mixed with earth, it no longer catches the sun's light; so likewise the human spirit or soul catches not God's light, unless it remain pure and set its desire upon that which is pure, viz. upon the light; for what life imaginates after, that it receives. The life of man is the form of the two inward worlds. If life desire sulphur in itself, then is Phur out of Sul its darkening; but if it desire only Sul, then it receives the power of the light, and in the power the light with its property. For in Phur, viz. in fierce wrathful Nature, life cannot remain clear as a mirror, but in Sul it can; for the life of man is a true mirror of the Deity, wherein God beholds himself. He gives his lustre and power to the human mirror, and finds himself in man, as also in angels and in the forms of heaven.

15. The light-world's essence is his finding or revelation, and the dark world's essence is his loss. He sees not himself in the dark world, for it has no mirror that were susceptible of the light. All that imaginates after the dark world's essence and property, that receives the dark world's property, and loses the mirror of God. It becomes filled with dark wrath; like as one mixes water with earth, and then the sun cannot shine therein. This water loses the mirror of the sun, and must withdraw again from the earth; else it is never-

more any mirror of the sun, but is imprisoned in the wrathful dark earth.

16. So it is also with human life. As long as it imaginates after God's Spirit, it receives God's power and light, and knows God. But when it imaginates after earthliness or after the dark world's property, it receives the essence of earthliness and of the dark world, and becomes filled with the same. Then is life's mirror shut up in darkness, and loses the mirror of God, and must be born anew.

17. As we know that Adam thus made the pure mirror earthly, and lost God's power and light, which Christ, God's Son, restored again, and broke open the earthly darkness, and forcibly introduced the mirror of God.

18. Thus we recognize how the holy tree grows through all things, and out of all beings; but is apprehended by no being, save only in the mirror of purity, as in the pure life of man; which life desires that tree, and it can be apprehended in no dark life. This then is the fourth point.

THE FIFTH POINT

How a life may perish in the tree of life.
How it passes out of the source of love
and joy into a source of misery, which
is contrary to all other lives.

CHAPTER VII

1. Every life is a clear gleam and mirror, and appears like a flash of a terrible aspect. But if this flash catch the light, it is transformed into gentleness and drops the terror, for then the terror unites itself to the light. And thus the light shines from the terrible flash; for the flash is the light's essence, it is its fire.

2. The flash contains the *centrum naturae*, being the fourth form of Nature where life rises, which in the steady fire, as in the principle, attains to perfection, but in the light is brought into another quality.

3. Now, the origin of the imagination [magical attraction] is in the first form of Nature, viz. in the desiring sourness, which carries its form through the dark world unto fire; for the first desire goes through all the forms, makes also all the forms, and is carried as far as to fire. There is the dividing bound-mark of spirit, there it is born. It is now free. It may by its imagination go back again into its mother the dark world, or, going forward,

sink down through the anguish of fire into death, and bud forth in the light. That depends on its choice. Where it yields up itself, there it must be; for its fire must have substance, that it may have something to feed upon.

4. Will the spirit eat of its first mother the sourness, that is, will it give to its fire for food the fierce essentiality in the centre, or the light's essentiality in the light-world, that is all in its own power; whatever its fire receives, in the property thereof does it burn.

5. In the dark property it burns in the dark, harsh, stern source, and sees in itself as a flash; it has only the mirror of darkness, and sees in the darkness. In the light's property it catches the gentleness of the light, in which the light-fire burns, and sees in the light-world. All is nigh unto spirit, and yet it can see in no other world or property save in that wherein its fire burns; of that world is the spirit only susceptible, it sees nothing in the other world; it has no eyes for that. It remains to it an eternal hiddenness, unless it has been in another world and gone out from thence, and given itself to another fire, as the devils did, who have indeed a knowledge of the light-world, but no feeling or seeing thereof; the light-world is nigh to them, but they know it not.

6. And now we are to recognize life's perdition, which comes about in the first Principle. There is the hinge, there the will may plunge whither it will. If it set its desire upon plurality and will itself be lord, then it cannot lay hold of plurality otherwise than in the dark, stern sour-

ness, in the dark world. But if it desire to plunge into the nothing, into freedom, it must abandon itself to fire; and then it sinks down in the death of the first principle, and buds forth out of the anguish of fire in the light. For when it abandons itself, the eternal will to Nature (which is God the Father) leads it out through fire into himself. For with the abandoning it falls unto the first will to Nature, who brings it by the other will, which is his Son or Heart, out of the anguishful Nature, and places it with the Son's will in freedom beyond the torment of fire. There it obtains, instead of plurality, all; not for its own glory or power, but for God's glory or power; God is in it both its will and its doing.

7. But whatever will itself be lord in fire, that goeth into its own number, into its essence which itself is; and whatever surrenders its power, surrenders also its fire-burning, and falls unto that which is a cause of fire, viz. unto the eternal will of God.

8. Thus it has fallen into freedom out of its fire of torment, and freedom kindles its fire. Its fire is now become a light and a clear mirror, for it has yielded itself up to Freedom, viz. to God. And thus its fire is a semblance and reflection of the Majesty of God.

9. But that which will not, but will itself be lord, that remains its own; it cannot bring itself in its own forms higher than to fire, moreover only to the flash; for no clear fire can burn in it, seeing it has in itself no clear substance for fire. The *centrum naturae* has nothing in itself from which a

clear brightness is able to arise ; but the freedom
out of Nature is a cause of such shining. Whatever
yields itself up to Nature, yet desires not Nature's
property but freedom, that becomes enkindled in
its flash of life by freedom, in the way the second
Principle has enkindled itself.

10. Thus we understand how a life perishes, that
is, how it introduces itself in anguish and torment
into darkness ; namely, when it will be its own lord
and desires plurality. If it will not give itself up
to death, then it cannot attain any other world.

11. For every life arises in the torment of anguish,
in Nature, and has no light in itself, except it enter
into that which gives birth to Nature ; there it
receives light.

12. For all that is in Nature is dark and in
anguish, as is to be recognized by this world. Were
the sun to be taken away, there would be nothing
but anguish and darkness. And therefore God put
himself in motion, so as to give a light to this world,
that the external life might be in light.

13. But as regards the inner life of the soul, it
has another form. This inner life can the external
not attain. Hath the soul's fire not God's light,
neither can the soul's will enter into God's light ;
it must remain in the darkness of the Eternal
Nature.

14. External Reason thinks, if the outward eye
sees, that is good ; there is no other seeing possible.
Bad enough, forsooth ! When the poor soul borrows
the external mirror, and must make shift with this
alone, where is its seeing ? When the external
mirror breaks, wherewith will it see then ? With

the terrible fire-flash in the horror, in the darkness ; it can see nowhere else.

15. Therefore it often happens when the poor captive soul beholds itself in the inward root, and thinks what will follow when for it the external mirror breaks, that it is terrified, and plunges the body in fear and doubt.

16. For it can look nowhere where its eternal rest might be, but it finds that it is in itself in utter unrest, moreover in a darkness; it has the external mirror only by way of loan.

17. As long as the soul is in this body, it may indeed make shift with the sun-mirror, for the sun has in its root the inner fire as the principle of the Father. From this fire the soul receives a lustre or mirror in the essence of the body, so that it is able thus in this earthly, transitory life to be in joy. But when the external mirror breaks, that is at an end ; and the soul's fire goes into the eternal house of mourning, into the centre of darkness.

18. The soul has in the time of the outer body three mirrors or eyes of all the three worlds. The mirror to which it turns itself, by that does it see. But it has no more than one as a natural right, namely the fire-flash, the fourth form of the dark world, where the two inward worlds separate (one into the darkness, the other into the light), and where its eternal origin is. The world into which the soul introduces its will, in the same it receives also substance, viz. a spiritual body. For this substance becomes for the soul's fire a food, or matter of its burning.

19. And therefore God has introduced the soul

into flesh and blood, that it might not so easily become susceptible of the wrath-essence. Thus it has its delight meanwhile in the mirror of the sun, and rejoices in the sidereal essence. Presented to it is (1) the light-world in its true fire, (2) the dark world in the fire-root, (3) the outer elemental world in the astral source. Among them hovers the great mystery of the soul's fire.

20. The world to which the soul unites and abandons itself, from that it receives substance in its imagination. But because it has in Adam turned itself to the spirit of this world, and carried its imagination into the same, its highest desire is now in the essence of the sun and stars, and by this desire it draws the spirit of the outer world with its substance of four elements continually into itself, and has its greatest joy therein; in which it is in a strange lodging as guest, for the abyss is beneath it, and there is great danger.

21. Here external Reason says: God has created the soul in flesh and blood in the outer world, what harm can that do it? This Reason knows no more of the soul's origin than a cow does of a new stable door. She looks at it, and it seems to her to be strange; so also to external Reason the inner world seems to be something strange.

22. It finds itself in the outer world, and aspires after that which the outer world has; and yet finds in itself the inner world, which continually arraigns the soul before God's wrath. It finds also the light-world, to which the inward desires of the soul's principle look. It feels indeed the longing after God, but the outer world hinders this and covers

it up; so that the desire after God's world cannot kindle fire in itself. If that were done, then would the light-world be manifest in the first principle, and the noble image of God would be revealed.

23. This is also hindered by the devil, who possesses the root of this world in the soul's fire. He is always holding up to the soul evil earthly things, or moving the root in the centre of Nature in the fierce wrath; so that the poor soul enkindles itself either in the wrath-fire in the evil poison-source, or else in fear and doubt of God's love. He has then carried the day, and sets before the soul external power, authority and honour, also the splendour and pomp of the outer world. Then the soul bites at this, and tickles itself therein with imagination ; and yet cannot truly enjoy the same, for it is only a borrowed mirror.

24. The poor soul is thus drawn away from God's light, and is sinking always into perdition, viz. into the dark house of misery, into the dark world. That did Adam prepare for us when he introduced his desire into earthliness. And thus the poor soul swims now in earthly flesh and blood, and is always eating of the tree of temptation of evil and good, and is drawn strongly by both ; and the serpent's monstrous shape is in the midst, in the source of wrath, and continually blows up the anger and fierce wrath.

25. Here then can the noble lily-branch nowhere recover itself, often also not recognize itself. It is oftentimes overwhelmed with the fierceness of malignity, so that it is as if it were wholly destroyed; and it would be destroyed were the mirror of the

Deity not turned towards it, in which the spirit of the will of the poor captive soul may recover itself, and regenerate itself therein.

26. For in the mirror of the light-world the incarnation of Christ is presented to the soul's spirit; and the Word that became man stands in sound, and is in action. Therein may the soul's spirit recover itself and generate itself anew; else it were often past help with the poor soul, when it is immersed in wrath and in the poison of the dark world.

27. And thus we understand at bottom what the destruction of the noble tree, or of the image of God, is, namely this:

28. The entire man is in his being the three worlds. The soul's centre, viz. the root of the soul's fire, contains the dark world; and the soul's fire contains the first Principle as the true fire-world. And the noble image, or the tree of divine growth, which is generated from the soul's fire and buds forth through fierce wrathful death in freedom or in the world of light, contains the light-world or the second Principle. And the body, which in the beginning was created out of the mixed substance which at creation arose from the light-world, the dark world and the fire-world, contains the outer world or the third mixed Principle.

29. The right soul is the spirit of these three worlds, as God's Spirit is the spirit of all the three worlds. In the dark world it is wrathful, stern and an austere source, and is called God's anger. In the light-world it is lovely, gentle and joyous, and is the spirit from God's heart, the Holy Spirit.

In the outer world it is the spirit of air, as also of fire and water, and may be used as man pleases, all unto the great wonders.

30. Thus is man according to the particular person the great mystery in the three worlds. The world to which he turns himself, in which he produces fruit, the same is lord in him, and this world becomes manifest in him; the other two remain hidden. As fire is hidden in wood, so light or the light-world remains hidden in the wrathful dark world; as also in malignity, in the distemper of the inner world in the outer world.

31. But if the light-world cannot become manifest in man so as to be lord, then the soul at the breaking of the outer world remains only in the dark world; for there it is no longer possible for the light-world to be kindled. There is for the light no longer any mirror that were turned towards the soul. The heart of God is not manifest therein, nor eternally can be (for the dark world must be, else the light would not be manifest); but here in this world that may be.

32. And though a soul be plunged in the deepest abyss, and lies in the wrath of God, yet in the external light of the sun it has before it the light-mirror wherein the divine power reveals itself, as also the mirror of the incarnation of Christ, which in the inner dark world never is known.

33. And our whole teaching is nothing else than how man should kindle in himself God's light-world. For if this be kindled, so that God's light shines in the soul's spirit, then the whole body hath light, as Christ says : If the eye be light, then is the whole

body light (Matt. vi. 22, 23).   He means the soul's
eye.   And if the wrath of the dark world be kindled,
then are body and soul dark, and have only a
lustre from the sun.   If the divine light be kindled,
it burns in love and meekness ; and if the wrath
of the dark world be kindled, it burns in stinging
envy and hate, in fierce rage, and flees away in the
external mirror of the sun's light into pride, and
will always be mounting above the source of love,
whereupon follows scorn and contempt of meekness
and of all that is lowly.

34. And here man should prove or try himself,
and recognize which world is lord in him.   If he
find that anger, wrath, envy, falsehood, lying and
deceit is his desire; also pride, avarice, and continual greed of honour and earthly pleasure, that
he is but a perpetual itch for wantonness and lewd-
ness ; then he may know with certainty that he
burns with anger, wrath, envy, falsehood, lying
and deceit in the dark, viz. in the dark world's
fire.   For this fire gives such essence, desire and
will.

35. And the other desire, viz. earthly pleasure,
pride, thirst for honour, avarice, and the perpetual
wanton bestial itch of concupiscence, is the fruit
which grows out of the dark world in the outer
world.

36. As love buds out of death (where the spirit of
the will yields up itself to the fire of God, and sinks
down as it were in death, but buds forth in God's
kingdom with a friendly desire always to do well);
so hath the will of wickedness given itself to perdition, viz. to wrathful, stern, eternal death, but

buds forth with its twig in this corrupt world in outer nature, and bears such fruit.

37. By this should every one learn to know himself, he need only search for his distinctive property. To whatever his will constantly drives him, in that kingdom does he stand ; and he is not a man as he accounts himself and pretends to be, but a creature of the dark world, viz. a greedy hound, a proud bird, a lustful animal, a fierce serpent, an envious toad full of poison. All these properties spring in him, and are his wood from which his fire burns. When the outer wood, or the substance of four elements, abandons him at his death, then the inner poisonous evil quality alone remains.

38. What figure now must stand in such a quality ? None else but what was strongest amongst these properties ; this is figured by the hellish *Fiat* in his form, as a venomous serpent, a dog or other beast. The property to which the spirit of the will has given itself up, that same property is afterward the soul's image. And this is one part.

39. Further, man should prove or try himself in his desire (for every man has these evil properties in him), to see whether he find in himself a constant longing to kill this poison and malignity ; whether he be enemy to this poison ; or whether he hath his delight in continually putting the false poison into operation, viz. in pride, covetousness, envy, licentiousness, lying and deceit.

40. Now, if he find in himself that he hath his delight therein, and is always ready to put the same into practice, then he is not a man, as he accounts himself to be ; but the devil in a strange

form deceives him, so that he believes he is a man. But he bears not God's but the serpent's image ; and is only in the external kingdom a likeness to an image of man, so long as he remains in this property, so that this property is supreme lord.

41. But if he find strife and combat within him, that his inner will always, yea hourly, fights against these evil properties, suppresses them, and suffers them not to attain to evil being ; that he would fain always do well, and yet finds that these evil properties hinder him, so that he cannot accomplish what he would ; and finds the desire for abstinence and repentance, that a perpetual desire after God's mercy springs in him, so that he would gladly do well if he could :

42. This man may think and assuredly know that God's fire glimmers in him, and continually labours towards the light. It would fain burn, and is always giving essence for flame ; but is quenched by the evil humidity of this world, which Adam has introduced into us.

43. But when the outer evil body with its vapours perishes, so that it can no longer obstruct the glimmering wick, then the divine fire becomes enkindled in its essence, and the divine image is figured according to the strongest quality which the man has here carried in his desire. If, however, he continue not in the above-mentioned warfare, but drops the struggle, he may again deteriorate most dangerously.

44. The third proof and trial is this, that a man recognize in what being or figure he stands. If he find that he hath a constant desire after God,

and in his desire is so strong that he can again break and transform into gentleness the evil essences, as often as for him a quality becomes enkindled ; that he is able to let all go that shines and glitters in this world ; that he can do good for evil ; that he hath full mastery over all his worldly substance, be it money or goods, to give thereof to the needy and for God's truth to abandon it all ; and freely and willingly for God's sake resign himself to misery in assured hope of that which is eternal : for him the divine power flows, so that he may kindle the light of the kingdom of joy therein ; he tastes what God is. He is the most undoubted man, and carries the divine image with heavenly essence in himself even in the time of the outer body.

45. There Jesus is born of the Virgin, and that man never dies. He lets pass from him only the earthly kingdom, which was to him in this time an opposition and hindrance, with which God has concealed him. For God will not cast pearls before swine ; they are hidden in Him.

46. This same new man dwells not in this world ; neither doth the devil know him, only he is hostile to his essence, which contains the inward centre ; for it impedes him that his will is not done. And therefore he incites the evil animal-men against him, to vex and persecute him, so that the true humanity remains concealed.

CHAPTER VIII

Of the right human essence from God's essence.

1. The right true human essence is not earthly, nor from the dark world; it is generated only in the light-world; it has no communion or fellowship with the dark world, nor with the outer world; there is a great bar, viz. death, between them.

2. Not that there is nothing of the true essence in the external man. It is there; for it was given to Adam in his image. But it is shut up and lies in death, and cannot qualify; neither has it any motion in itself, unless it become quick in the power of the Deity. As it became quick in the Virgin Mary by God's motion and entrance; there the right human essence came again to life.

3. So also in us the right human essence is not stirring, except we be born of God in Christ.

4. In the baptism of infants the Word of God enters into union and connection with them in the covenant, and is the first stirring in this world; as a smouldering in wood that begins to glimmer, but the wicklet is often after darkened and extinguished. Moreover, in many a child that is begotten of wholly godless essence, it is not susceptible.

5. Christ said: Suffer little children to come unto me, for of such is the kingdom of God (Mark x. 14). Not dogs, wolves, toads or serpents, but children, in whom the essence is not wholly devilish. For

many a child is baptized in the wrath of God, for which the parents are to blame. An evil tree bears evil fruit, says Christ.

6. And though He is come into this world to save what was lost, yet it depends also on the essence of that which will let itself be helped. For an animal-man may attain the image [of God], if he turn round and suffer the Word that became man to draw him. If not, then he remains in his animal essence an evil beast.

7. But we are not to suppose that baptism lays the first foundation of the human essence, and is wholly the first enkindling cause of the divine fire. No, that is not so; for a child becomes through the parents' essence a spirit, as also flesh and blood, with espousal of the constellation of the spirit *majoris mundi.*

8. At the time when a child in the womb has attained to life, then immediately divine or hellish essence glimmers from the primal fount and origin.

9. And if but a small spark of the divine essence be active, the child is susceptible of baptism. And though it should die unbaptized, yet the spark is in God's Mystery, and glimmers in God's kingdom, and is kindled in the fire of God. For it dies in the Mysterium of the Father, and glimmers up in the Mysterium of the Son who became man.

10. The parents' baptism and covenant is its baptism and covenant. The reconciliation has taken place in human blood, in the right true human essence. God's word or heart has given itself to the shut up, dead, human essence; not to the earthly part, but to the heavenly part.

Not to the part that Adam by his imagination introduced, which is earth; but to the part which was given to Adam from the angelic world, which he corrupted and poisoned with the earthly craving, for in the craving earthly, coarse, animal flesh was produced.

11. This part has the right human essence, and in this part God became man. And this same part has the ground of the angelic world, for it takes its origin from the angelic world.

12. But if most frequently godless parents are immersed wholly in the wrath of God, and so beget children in the wrath; then is their seed shut up in death, and has in it nothing of the right human essence, which is moving, save only what the constellation in the spirit *majoris mundi* has in itself. There certainly the divine power has some movement; but the wrath's power exists as opposite, and is heavy. Nevertheless, there is no impossibility; for the incarnation of God, his becoming man, is presented to all souls in the life's light.

13. But baptism contains something else. God's essence (as the water of eternal life born of God's gentleness) must move the right human essence (with Adam shut up in death), and yield itself up there as a new life or a living essence. God's water must baptize; the Holy Spirit must be the operant.

14. But I say, according to my knowledge, that the water of eternal life, upon which the Holy Spirit broods, will hardly yield itself up to the poison of wrath and death, where there is not an essence of desire [toward God].

15. I say, then, that a child (as soon as it has life in the womb) is, so far as the divine essence is moving in the heavenly part, already baptized by the Holy Spirit, and attains the incarnation of Christ. For baptism depends not on the priest's power, that the Holy Spirit should wait upon him. The incarnation of Christ waited not upon man's power, but upon the goal that God set in his covenant. This goal was blessed. Therefore the angel said to Mary : Blessed art thou among women. The goal lay in her, and was blessed, and blessed her also when God's heart awakened the goal.

16. This goal reached back to Adam, and forward to the last man. When God became man, the goal was awakened in the heavenly part ; not only in Mary, but also in Adam and Eve, and all their children who had given themselves up to God ; these were all blessed in the goal.

17. For that is the covenant of grace which God established with Adam and Eve. This covenant is in all human essence, but not in devilish essence.

18. But baptism is the seal that God affixed to the covenant, as in the old testament circumcision. In baptism God gives divine water to the human race as a pledge and seal ; but the covenant is already there before baptism ; it was made in paradise, yea before the foundation of the world. As soon as a soul is stirring in the womb, so that a human soul is born, it is in the covenant. For Christ has given himself to the fire of God, to the principle, and fulfilled the covenant, and is become the result of the testament.

19. This result waits not upon any external ordinance, upon the delusion of the outer man; but as soon as a soul is born from the principle, it is in the result of the testament, so far as the divine life is moving in it. But not in godless souls; in them the divine life must first be born. God's wrath swallows up many a soul still in essence, before it attains the principle; because it is from false essence, from evil seed of the parents.

20. Reason says: What can a child do to this, that the parents are wicked? Nay, what can even God do? It is in the parents' power to get a child. What can God do to this, that whores and profligates creep together? Though the false tree springs not thus from this line only, but also in marriage. Man is free; if he awaken no life, his seed remains an essence. Shall God, because of the child's innocency, cast pearls before swine? The kingdom of heaven confronts it; let it enter, God closes the kingdom of heaven to none.

21. But a bad man is shut up in body and soul, why not also in the seed? The seed is truly the fruit of his body. If we would reap good wheat, we of right sow wheat; but if thistle seed be sown, a thistle grows from it. Must God then change that into wheat? Has not the sower power to sow in his field what he pleases? Or wilt thou say: What can the thistle do to this, that it is a thistle and pricks? It belongs not among the wheat, but grows up itself along with it.

22. God were certainly content though no thistle-child did grow; it is not his ordinance. But the devil sows weeds amongst the wheat, viz. in the

heart of man. Why does man suffer this and destroy himself, so that his essence becomes a thistle-seed, and yields weeds to the fire in the wrath of God? It is not all attributable to the seed, but depends on the field. Many a noble grain perishes in the evil field's essence. The heavens with the sun give life and power to all growth. The sun makes no weeds, neither desires any; but the essence in the field makes oftentimes another thing, and destroys the good.

23. So also in man. Many a curse sticks which one wishes the other, when the other has provoked it, and is apt for it; as indeed is common among godless married people, one wishing the other the devil and hell-fire. If then they both be godless, should not then their godless will be realized to them, by their begetting godless children? There is not anything that is good in them, what good thing then shall come out of them? What can God do to this? He sets his word and teaching before them, and announces to them their destruction. If they will not regard it, let them go whither they please. So too is their seed; and thus many a child is born a thistle and evil beast, and is baptized in the wrath of God.

24. For, of what essence the soul's spirit is, in such an essence it receives also the divine nature in the covenant: one in the power of light, in love; another in the power of wrath, in darkness.

25. The covenant at baptism stands firm. Every child is baptized in the covenant; the Spirit of God baptizes each one, if we observe the customary form, but in accordance with the child's property.

Often the father and mother, as also the baptizer, are godless, and only evil beasts, and there is no real earnestness. The outward pomp and the money is the main point with them; they despise the mystery. Here the child is wholly in the property of wrath. Who then shall baptize? None other than the wrath of God in his covenant, for that men do but make a mock of it.

26. Thus the source of wrath seizes the new spirit, works powerfully in it, and brings forth fruit to perdition. As St. Paul says of the other testament, that the wicked man receives it unto judgment, not discerning the Lord's body (1 Cor. xi. 29). That is, he distinguishes not in himself the heavenly part of his essence from the earthly, to put his will into the heavenly and offer this up to God; but deems all common, as an ox eats the fodder.

27. Therefore the wrath of God springs in him, so that he doth not break off his will from the earthly and repent of his wickedness. His heavenly part cannot become partaker of God's body, because he cannot awaken the essence of the heavenly part. Thus it has no mouth to receive God's body, the mouth being shut up in death. The earthly part, however, receives Christ's body, but according to the property of wrath, according to the property of the dark world; for the testament must stand.

28. In like manner in baptism. According as the soul's essence is in being, so also does it enjoy God's covenant. It were better a wholly godless child were not baptized, and that a wicked man in his sins without conversion did not touch God's

testament; for it brings them both only power to perdition. God's covenant is never moved without fruit. God works in his covenant according to his word.

29. As is the soul which moves the covenant, so is the medicament in the covenant, and in such a power the Spirit of God works in love and wrath; for he is the spirit of every life, and assimilates himself to every life. He is in every thing as the thing's will and property is, for one property seizes the other. What the soul wills, that he wills also, and thereinto the soul enters.

30. It is all magical; what the will of a thing wills, that it receives. A toad takes only poison into itself, though it sit in the best apothecary's shop; the like also does a serpent. Every thing takes only its own property into itself; and though it eat the substance of a good property, yet it converts all in itself into its own property. Though a toad should eat honey, yet this becomes poison in it. As indeed the devil was an angel; but when he willed nothing good, his heavenly essence became to him hellish poison, and his evil will remained evil one time as another.

31. We are therefore highly to consider our life, what we would do and be at. We have evil and good in us. The one wherein we draw our will, its essence becomes active in us; and such a property we draw also from without into us. We have the two Mysteries, the divine and the devilish in us, of the two eternal worlds, and also of the outer world. What we make of ourselves, that we are; what we awaken in ourselves, that is moving

in us. If we lead ourselves to good, then God's
Spirit helps us ; but if we lead ourselves to evil,
then God's wrath and anger helps us. Whatever
we will, of that property we obtain a leader, and
thereinto we lead ourselves. It is not God's will
that we perish, but his wrath's and our own will.

And thus we understand the fifth point. How
a life perishes, and how out of good an evil comes,
and out of evil a good, when the will turns round.

THE SIXTH POINT

CHAPTER IX

1. The life of darkness is repugnant to all life of light; for the darkness gives fierce and hostile essence, and the life of light gives love-essence.

2. In the darkness there is in the essence only a perpetual stinging and breaking, each form being enemy to the other—a contrarious essence. Each form is a liar to itself, and one says to the other, that it is evil and adverse to it, that it is a cause of its restlessness and fierceness. Each thinks in itself: If only the other form were not, thou wouldst have rest; and yet each of them is evil and false. Hence it is, that all that is born of the dark property of wrath is lying, and is always lying against the other forms, saying they are evil; and yet it is itself a cause thereof, it makes them evil by its poisonous infection.

3. Thus are they all, and lying is their truth. When they speak lies, they speak from their own forms and properties. And so also are their creatures. Therefore Christ said: The devil is a liar and murderer from the beginning (John viii.

44). For each form desires to murder the other, and yet there is no killing; but the greater the strife is, the greater becomes their murderous life.

4. And therefore it is called an eternal death and enmity, where nothing but contrariety arises. For there is nothing that could abolish the strife, nothing that could hold in check a single form. The more it were resisted, the greater would be the fierceness; like a fire that is stirred, whereby it burns but the more.

5. Thus the fierce wrathful kingdom can be extinguished by nothing, save only by God's light, by which it becomes wholly gentle, lovely and full of joy. And neither can that be; for if the dark kingdom were to be kindled with the light, the light would have no root to its nature and property, no fire could be generated, neither were there any light, nor any power, but all were a nothing.

6. Hence the kingdom of wrath must be, for it is a cause of the fire-world and light-world, and all is God's. But all is not acknowledged as or called God, as the dark world has another property, and the light-world is a cause of the fierceness and terror of the dark property; for the darkness is terrified at the light, and stands in eternal terror because the light-world dwells in it. It trembles eternally before the light, and yet cannot apprehend it; but is only a cause of life and of movement. And thus all must be subservient to the glory of God.

7. The life of darkness has many forms; it is not one and the same property. As we are to recognize by the creatures of this world, where one

is always worse than the other, also has its subsistence in a different source from the other; who nevertheless all live in the sun's power and light, by which they are meekened.

8. But if the sun were to be extinguished, then would the deep be wrathful and stinging. Then we should soon see the property of the dark world, how all creatures would become poisonous and evil.

9. For every life is rooted in poison. The light alone resists the poison, and yet is a cause that the poison lives and faints not.

10. We are therefore to recognize that the life of darkness is only a fainting poison, like a dying source; and yet there is no dying there. For the light - world stands opposed to the mirror of darkness, whereby the darkness is eternally in terror.

11. The dark life is like a terror, where the flash and terror is always mounting upwards, as if it would quit the life and fly out above it. And hence arises pride, so that the devil is always wishing to be above God; it is his proprium, his life's figure is so, and he cannot do otherwise. Just as a poison rages and pierces, as if it would break loose from the member;

12. So is the life of darkness in itself. The poisonful essences make such an inward disposition, and from the disposition proceeds such a will-spirit. There is such a property therein, and consists of seven forms, according to the centre of Nature with its principle. As the life of joy consists of seven forms by right of Nature, so also

does the life of sorrowfulness. That which in the light gives joy, in the darkness gives sorrowfulness.

13. And yet it is not to be thought that the life of darkness therefore sinks down into misery, that it would forget itself as if it were sorrowful. There is no sorrowing; but what with us on earth is sorrowing according to this property, is in the darkness power and joy according to the property of the darkness. For sorrowfulness is a thing that is swallowed up in death. But death and dying is the life of the darkness, just as anguish is the life of the poison. The greater the anguish becomes in the poison, the stronger becomes the poison-life, as is to be seen in the external poison.

14. We cannot, then, say of the devil that he sits in dejection, as if he were faint-hearted. There is no faint-heartedness in him, but a constant will to kindle the poison-source more, that his fierceness may become greater. For this fierceness is his strength, wherein he draws his will to mount above the thrones and inflame them. He would be a mighty lord in the poison-source, for it is the strong and great life. But the light is his misery and dread; that checks his bravery. He is terrified at the light; for it is his true poison, which torments him. Because he abandoned it, it now resists him. Of which he is ashamed, that he is thus a deformed angel in a strange image. He would be content with the source of wrath, if only the light were not so near him. Shame is therefore so great in him that he grows furious, and kindles his poisonous source more and more, so that his

figure becomes increasingly horrible, and the divine image is not recognized in him. He aims only at how he may storm and rage against God, as if he were a foreign thing, or a foreign power, as if he had a foreign kingdom; whereas he is poor, and the dark kingdom is not his, but he is only a prisoner in it. It is God's abyss; he is only a creature therein. He would be lord therein, and yet is but a juggler with the fierceness; although he must act according to the property. And this is also a wonder before the stern might of eternity. It is as a sport wherewith the stern might hath its dissipation, by which it is distinguished what evil or good, joy or sorrow, is; and that the creatures in the light-world have cause to humble themselves. And yet God created no devil, nor destined Lucifer for the dark world. But this is enmity in Lucifer, that he was an angel, and that the light is so near him that he became an apostate.

15. There is no pain in the creatures which have been created in the dark world; for they are of the fierce wrathful property, and know nothing of the light. Fierceness is their strength and might, and enmity their will and life. The more evil and hostile a creature is in the dark world, the greater is its might. As the powerful tyrants of this world often exhibit their power in malignity, so that men must fear them, or as tame animals are afraid of ferocious ones; so has this likewise a property in the dark world.

16. If we will rightly consider the property of the dark world, let us look upon the malice and

pride of this world, which is a figure or type. For all malice, falsehood, pride and covetousness has its root from the dark world ; it is the property of the dark world, whether it be recognized in men or beasts.

17. For this world rests upon the foundation of the dark world. The dark world gives to this world essence, will and quality. And had not the good been introduced also at creation, there would be no other doing or will in this world than in the dark world. But the divine power and the sun's light hinder that. As is to be seen among men and beasts, how there is a biting, hating and striking, and an arrogant self - will, each wishing to rule over the other, to kill and devour the other, and elevate itself alone ; also to trample upon everything with guile, wrath, malice and falsehood, and make itself lord.

18. In like manner the dark world has such a property. What all wicked men in this world do in their malice and falsehood, that also the devils do in the dark world ; and what the poisonous evil worms and beasts in their malignity do, that also the other creatures do in the dark world. Though they are without such a body, yet they have such a property in their spiritual body ; and though they have a body, yet it is after the fashion of spirit, as the devils have one.

19. The birth, being, essence and dominion of the dark world lies principally in the first four forms of Nature, viz. in the source of anguish, in an exceedingly strong and powerful dominion, where all in the essence is divulged. For gentleness

is the enmity of the wrath-power, and each is against the other.

20. Else, if they should be one, there would necessarily be but one quality ; and if there were also only one will, the eternal wonders could not become manifest. But the manifold quality makes the eternal wonders manifest. For eternity could not otherwise become manifest, nor attain to being, save through the enkindling, viz. in the stern harsh attraction in which the dark world stands, and in which the fire-world and also the light-world take their rise. All is only a single essence or substance, but it separates itself into three properties. One property is not separated from the other, but each gives the other ; as is to be seen in fire and light, as also in the matter from which the fire burns.

21. And man need not search deeper, for he is himself the essence of all beings. But because he has in his creation turned aside from his original order, and introduced and awakened another quality in himself, it is necessary for him to inquire how he may re-enter into his eternal order and quality, and generate himself anew. And then, how he may extinguish the fierce wrathful quality which is moving in him, for all is active in him and draws him, both evil and good. Therefore he should learn how to resist wrath, and walk in meekness, in the quality of light and of love.

22. Man, moreover, has no law except he enkindle himself in the dark world's property, and walk according to this property. Independently of that, all is free to him. Whatsoever he doth in meekness and love is without restriction for him, and is his

proper being; it consists not in any one's name or presumption.

23. All that is grown from one root is and belongs to one tree, it is but one manner of fruit; unless it corrupt itself, so that the very essence changes.

24. As long as a thing remains in the essence from which it arose, it has no law; but if it withdraw therefrom into another quality, the first quality hangs unto it, and is in conflict with the other. And then law ensues, that it should return again into that which it originally was, and be one, not two; for one thing should exercise only one dominion, not two. Man was created in the dominion of love and gentleness, as in God's Being, and therein he was to remain.

25. But because he has awakened another dominion, viz. fierce wrath, he is now in combat and strife, and has laws, that he may mortify and abandon the fierceness, and be in one dominion again. Since then both dominions are become powerful in him, and the dominion of wrath has overpowered love, he must wholly break to pieces in substance, and be re-born again from the first root. And therefore he has in this twofold being laws, how he should conduct himself and generate a will-spirit unto the eternal dominion.

26. All this lies in his power. He may bring forth the spirit of wrath or the spirit of love, and in accordance with the same he is separated whither and into which world he belongs; for he separates himself.

27. But the law continues over him as long as he

is in this life (field). Then, when the weed separates from this field of the body, it is in one dominion again, where it shall remain eternally; for after that there is nothing more to give it law, inasmuch as it is wholly one in its will, either to do evil or good.

28. But in this external life man is in combat and strife. Two dominions, qualities and laws repose in him. The divine unto love and righteousness; and the wrathful in the rising of pride in the power of fire, in the stern, harsh, hellish covetousness, envy, anger and malice. The one to which the spirit unites itself, of that dominion it is. The other hangs unto it, and reproaches it to its face as a perjured wretch and an apostate; but nevertheless draws it, and will have it. Thus life is in a desperate strait between the two, and is at odds with itself.

29. But if it resolve rashly, and abandon itself wholly to the wrath, then the fierce wrath destroys the first image according to God. And if it cannot entirely, because the divine power hinders that, then it would cast the whole man headlong; and many a one is plunged into despair in this anguish, so that he lays violent hands on himself.

30. Thus the soul with the image falls unto the wrathful, dark world; and the image is brought into a hellish figure, into a form of its property which it had here. So it fared also with the devils, who have lost their first image.

31. Every devil has an image according to his property, according to the figure of the wrath, in accordance with its quality; like as there are

horrible worms or evil beasts, and such a thing has also the lost soul to expect.

32. External Reason supposes that hell is far from us. But it is near us. Every one carries it in himself, unless he kill the hellish poison with God's power, and bud forth therefrom as a new twig, which the hellish quality cannot seize or touch (*rügen*).

33. Though indeed the fierceness of hell is recognized more in one place than in another, all according to the hellish dominion, where the upper dominion is powerful in various places in the locus of this world; all according to the first enkindling of King Lucifer, as in many places of the earth, as also in the deep between the stars and the earth, is the hellish quality to be discerned above other places, where the inner fierceness extends to the external principle. Here then are distinct dominions of devils, also of the other hellish properties; here the fierce wrath of God has strongly inflamed itself, and now burns until the judgment of God.

34. Every man carries heaven and hell within him in this world. The property which he awakens, the same burns in him, and of that fire is the soul susceptible. And when the body dies, the soul needs to go nowhither, but it is committed to the hellish dominion of which it is the property. Those devils who are of its property await it, and receive it into their dominion until the judgment of God. And though they are confined to no place, yet they belong to the same dominion, and the same quality they have everywhere. Wherever they

go, they are in the same dominion and quality;
for the abyss has no place, neither time nor space.
As it was before the times of the world, when there
was no place; so it is and remains so eternally
in the abyss.

35. And though the place of this world was
given to Lucifer for a kingdom (for he was created
therein), yet he has been cast out from place and
position, and dwells in the abyss, where he can
never reach any place of the angelic kingdom; but
is shut up in his own realm in the abyss, where he
must bear eternal reproach as a prisoner. As is
done to a malefactor, who is put into a dark dungeon
away from all the beings of this world, where he
must do without any mundane joy or pleasure,
and bear the reproach of his crime.

36. So it fares also with the devils, and with
all damned souls, who lie captive in the dark prison.
Nor do they desire to come out, because of the
great reproach of their horrible form and image.
And wherever they go, yet they never enjoy any
good; there is among them no refreshment. But
they lie in hell as the dead, or as eternally hungry,
fainting and thirsty; and are only an evil poison-
source. All is to them adverse and contrary.
They have only a thirst after anguish and malice;
these they devour eternally, and bring forth
blasphemies upon themselves. The more horrible
they can make their figure, the more pleasing
that is to them. Like buffoons, who on earth
would fain be always the greatest fools, give themselves a hideous appearance, and have their delight
therein; so they do also eternally in hell, and

accordingly they begin the game here on earth. As the tyrant delights when he can torment men, and spend their sweat in show and luxury, in foolish strange attire and behaviour, and ape the fool; so do also the devils in hell. And the luxury of this world in its strange garb is a true type of the hellish world.

37. All the curious tassels and tufts which the proud man devises, and clothes his foolish man therewith, whereby he would be distinguished from the true children of God, are types of the hellish world. All his bedizenment, glittering show and ostentation, by which he withdraws himself from humility, is a hellish mirror; for the devil's pride will be like to none, it keeps itself distinct in this world. And the blind man understands not this, how the devil fools and deceives him, and thus only to mock God prefigures his own proud mask; so that the poor man does as he does, and thinks he is thereby fine, and better than other men, whereas we all arise and proceed from one body and spirit. But before God and his angels he is recognized only as a devil's mask, and is in the sight of heaven an abomination. As a fool in comparison with wisdom is but an abomination, so is also hypocritical pride an abomination before God and his angels, in presence of the noble image. The world still cleaves to this abomination, and therewith marks out the corrupt image of earthliness.

38. He who sees a proud man sees the heavy fall of Adam, and a type of the hellish world; a half devil and half man, to whom the devil has continual access. For he is the devil's servant in this

world ; the devil does his work through him, and the poor man knows it not, and so enters the devil's service to his eternal reproach. He thinks he is thereby fine and important, and is thereby in the sight of God only as a fool, who puts on strange clothing and takes to himself animal form.

CHAPTER X

Of the four elements of the devil and of the dark world; how we shall know them in this outer world.

1. The first element of the dark world and of the devil is pride, the second covetousness, the third envy, the fourth anger. These four elements are everlastingly hatching a young son, who is called Falsehood. This son is also a true son of the corrupt Adam, whom he left behind him to be a lord of the world. He has become king in the world, and has possessed the whole world, and rules everywhere in the third principle. Whoever rightly knows this king, knows the four elements of the devil; for in the dark world these four elements have entire dominion in spirit and body, and in all that is called being.

2. And we see hereby clearly that this world rests upon the foundation of these four elements, and receives from them tendency, quality and will. For the son of these four elements rules on earth; he will have all obedient under him, and has four different races of his subjects. (1) The race of pride, which will be above all other, and will put itself on a level with none. (2) The race of covetousness, which will alone possess all, subdue all under it, and will have all. This second race is the son of the first, for pride will also have all, that it alone may be all. (3) The third race is envy,

which is the son of covetousness. When it sees
it cannot alone have all, it stings like a poison, and
begrudges anything to any one. Its will in all
things is either to draw to itself and possess alone,
or to rage therein with an evil will. (4) The fourth
race is anger, which is the son of envy. What it
cannot attain with evil will, that it enkindles in the
fire of wrath, and breaks it by force. It brings
about war and slaughter, and would destroy everything. This race would subdue all by violence.

3. These, then, are the four elements of the
devil, all which four are in one another as one.
One proceeds from the other, and one gives birth
to the other. They take their origin from the dark
Nature, viz. from sour, bitter, anguish and fire.

4. But seeing God's power is for them an opposition, so that in this world they have not full
dominion, they have generated a crafty son, by
whom they rule, who is called Falsehood. He takes
the coat of divine colours upon him, that he may
not be known; and wishes to be called a son of
truth and virtue, but is an impostor. He speaks
in one way, and thinks and acts in another. He
carries the lustre of God on his tongue, and the
devil's power and poison in his heart.

5. This is king on earth, and manages two kingdoms. The first is called perdition; the second
Babel, a confusion. The kingdom of perdition
this king has clothed with strength and might; it
is the garment of that kingdom. On the other
kingdom, Babel, he has put a white shining garment. That must be to it in place of God, and with
that the king rules on earth as if he were God. And

the people worship this garment; and beneath it
is the man of falsehood and deceit, and hath in him
his mother the four elements, viz. pride, covetousness, envy and anger.

6. Thus the four elements of the devil rule under
a hypocritical coat, and men strive eagerly for this
coat. Every one will put it on; but he who puts it on,
puts on hell and God's wrath. This coat is honoured
in God's stead, and is the coat which the wrath
of God did put on Adam and Eve, when the devil
deceived them, so that they fell from obedience to
God. And it is the very same coat of which God
from the beginning of the world has warned us,
that we should not put it on; for the devil has
his lodging in it. When we put it on, we take up
our abode with the devil, and must do what he
pleases; for he is host in that house, and rests in
that coat.

7. Because he is a prisoner of God, he puts his
coat on us, and sends us therewith to Babel into
his service, where we cannot but mock God; for
we have on God's coat, and the devil lodged under
it as guest. Thus the tongue gives God good words,
and the heart has the spirit of the four elements
of wrath; and God is therefore mocked by the
devil, that God shall see that he, the devil, is lord
and king over men, and esteems God's dominion
in man only as a shining coat, in which he, the devil,
is man, and has man captive in his arms. He covers
him indeed with the coat, and allows man to call
himself God's child; but in this coat man does only
his will for him, so that all that the devil cannot or
may not do in the external kingdom, that man does

for him in his service. The devil may not kill
any one, and man does it readily to please him.
Neither can the devil use God's creatures, and
man misuses them willingly to please him, thereby
to mock God. With this he practises pride and
covetousness, also falsehood and malice, and accomplishes by them all that the devil would have; he
shines also therewith as if he were God.

8. The external kingdom is therefore become a
perpetual murderous den of the devil. The false
and pretended man (who calls himself a man, but is
not) does the butchery, and increases God's wrath,
and kindles the dark world in this outer world, so
that God's wrath continually burns in this world.

9. Thus God's kingdom is hindered, and the
devil's will done; and the devil remains a prince
on earth, whereas otherwise he could accomplish
nothing on earth. The pretended man is in his
service, and does his will. Two species of men,
then, dwell together on earth. The one are real
true men, who serve God in the coat of humility
and misery, whom the devil derides and torments
them with the other species, and in their case
brings all his wonders to pass by means of those
who serve him.

10. The other species also calls itself men, walk
also in human form, but they are evil beasts. They
put on the garment of their King, that is to say,
Falsehood; and live in the power of the four
elements of their king, viz. in pride, covetousness,
envy and anger.

11. Pride is the first virtue. It snatches the
bread from the mouth of the real man, and coerces

the wretched, that it may satisfy itself. It insists
that nothing shall be on a level with it; it will
be alone the fairest child in the house. It has put
on the coat of dissimulation, and would be called
righteous; people must honour it and bow themselves before it. Nothing must compare itself to
it. It will be lord, and says: I am modest in my
demeanour.

12. But its heart is covetousness. That is the
wolf, and devours the sweat and labour of the
wretched. Pride mounts up above all. It explores
daily the wonders of God, to see how it may dis-
semble and play the hypocrite. It affects to be
friendly and chaste, as if it were a virgin full of
modesty; and yet is a strumpet full of flaws, and
at heart hates all virtue, chastity and righteousness. It is a perpetual enemy of love and humility.
Whatever is simple, that it despises; and yet
forces the simple under its yoke. It says to the
real true man : Thou art my dog, I will hunt thee
whither I list. Thou art foolish, and I am wise;
and it is itself the biggest fool. It forfeits God and
the kingdom of heaven for a little while's delight of
the eyes; it plunges itself into darkness, and puts
on the coat of anxiety.

13. The second virtue of this King Falsehood
is covetousness. This draws all to itself, and
darkens the shining adornment of pride. It draws
to itself evil and good promiscuously, and continually fills pride full. And when it has filled it, it
takes its son envy and torments pride therewith,
so that it has no rest in its splendour. Envy
stings incessantly in the desiring covetousness, as

if it were mad and frantic; and tortures pride day and night, so that it never rests. Covetousness is the right coarse swinish beast; it desires more than it can eat. Its jaws are wide open day and night. It suffers not man to rest, and torments him continually in its sordid filthiness, so that he has an eager longing earthward, and toward the things the earth yields without any one's covetousness; only labour belongs thereto, and no covetousness.

14. Covetousness plagues itself and is its own enemy; for it fills itself with pain and disquietude, and clouds man's understanding, so that he cannot recognize that all comes from the divine hand. It makes dark for man his life's light, consumes the body, and robs him of the divine senses and glory. It casts him into the pit of death, and brings him temporal and eternal death. It attracts dark matter into man's noble image, and makes of an angel a fierce wrathful devil. It creates the *turba* in body and soul, and is the horrible beast in the abyss of hell, for it is the cause of suffering and pain; without it no pain could arise. It causes war and strife, for it is never satisfied. If it had all the world, it would want to have also the abyss; for there is no place made for its rest. It builds up countries and kingdoms, and destroys them also again. It drives man into mere trouble and turmoil; it is simply the devil's heart and will.

15. For pride is the brave spirit which grows from covetousness. It is the fair child that was to possess heaven; but covetousness has trans-

formed it into a bastard-child, and has introduced
it into Babel, into the mother of the great whoredom on earth. There pride continually prosti-
tutes itself to covetousness, and is but a bastard-
child in the sight of God. It cannot possess
heaven; it has its kingdom of heaven on earth.
It makes court to King Falsehood, who takes all
its labour, and gives it to the four elements of the
devil in the dark world; and thither must pride
follow also with covetousness, when the bag of
anxious avarice breaks. The same is indeed so
very just, and yet takes its covetousness with it
into the abyss, that pride may have its delight
therein. As a fool in his fool's dress, who toils
and vexes himself that he may bring forth folly
and please his spectators, that he may be an
extravagant fool; so in like manner pride and
covetousness is God's fool and the devil's juggler,
who hath his delight in this, that he can make of
God's image a fool's image.

16. The third virtue is envy, in the four elements of the devil, in the kingdom of falsehood.
The same is a sting, a rager and raver, like an evil
poison. It can abide nowhere, and has no resting-
place. Its mother covetousness allows it no rest;
it must always rage and rave. It must enter into
that in which it is not generated. It is the mouth
of covetousness, a perpetual liar and slanderer.
It pierces into its neighbour's heart, and wounds it.
It devours itself for very poisonful hunger, and yet
never has enough. It causes restlessness without
limit or measure. It is the greatest poison and the
eye of hell, whereby the devil sees in the soul and

body of man. Nothing is like unto it. It is no
fire, but the sting of fire. It brings about all
ill, and yet finds no rest ; the more it pushes on,
the more frantic it is. It is a famished poison.
It needs no being, and yet rages in being. It
makes man more than mad, so that he desires
to storm and rave against God. It is the essence
of hell and of wrath, and makes of love the greatest
enmity. It grudges any one anything, and yet is
itself a starved nothing.

17. Envy is the devil's will-spirit ; and the man
who takes it as a lodging, receives the devil and
God's wrath ; for it brings hellish torture and
pain. It is the eternal hostile torment and unrest,
and destroys the noble image of God ; for it is the
enemy of God and of all creatures.

18. The fourth virtue, in the four elements in
the kingdom of falsehood of the devil, is anger,
rage. This is the right hell-fire ; for anger is
generated between covetousness and envy. It is
the fire and life of envy. What envy cannot do,
that anger accomplishes. Anger takes body and
soul together, and runs like a raging devil. It
would destroy and shatter everything ; it runs
against walls and strongholds. And though it
burst itself, still it is furious, like a mad dog that
bites and kills all ; and is so venomous in its wrath,
that, what it cannot overpower, it nevertheless
poisons. This is the true podagra of the world.
When pride in its hypocritical coat cannot get the
mastery by guile and falsehood, it must then give
effect to the fourth virtue, which strikes with the
fist and brings about war. Oh, how merry is the

devil when his four elements rule thus ! He still thinks he is lord on earth. For though he is a prisoner, yet the animal-men perform his office well ; and accordingly he holds men in derision, that they are and do worse than he himself can do.

19. These are, then, the four elements of the dark world, in which the devil opines to be a God ; and therewith he rules on earth by his faithful son Falsehood. This latter is the smug kitling, who before gives good words, and yet always has the mouse in view. Can it but catch it : Oh, how brisk and jocund it is when it can bring the roast meat to the devil ! With these four elements man is surrounded, and lodges in the country of the false king. They shoot him at all hours to the heart, and would destroy his noble image. He must always be at war against them, for they lodge with him and in him; they make thrusts continually at him, and would destroy his choicest jewel.

20. If but one of these four elements obtain in man power to qualify, this one enkindles all the others ; and they straightway rob him of his noble image, and make of him a mask of the devil. And no man who allows to these four elements power to qualify can with truth say of himself, that he is a man ; for he qualifies into the devil's property, and is an enemy of God. And though the devil clothe him with the hypocritical coat, so that he is able to give good words and knows how to be elegant in his manners, that men think he is a child of God, yet he is not a man as long as these four elements have the upper-hand in him; but he is a diabolized man, half devil and half man,

till he make his measure full : then he is an entire
devil in human shape.

21. Let every one, therefore, learn to know
himself,—what kind of properties rule in him. If
he find that all these four elements, or one only,
rule in him, he has to take the field against them,
or it will turn out ill in the end. He will not be
permitted to comfort himself with the kingdom of
heaven. Only let him not suffer the devil to wrap
him round with the hypocritical cloak, as happens
when men live in these four elements, and subtly
flatter themselves with the sufferings of Christ.
That must be the covering of this impostor. The
impostor might retain his dominion, if he did not
tickle himself with Christ's satisfaction.

22. Oh, how the shining coat of Christ will be
stript off thee! Then will be seen standing in
Babel the whore with the four virtues. It is not
merely a question of taking comfort, but of keep-
ing down the impostor, lest he become master in
the house. He must not bear rule, but righteousness, love, humility and chastity, and constant
cheerful well-doing. Not dissembling and giving
good words, but doing. There must be doing : viz.
striving against the devil's will, contenting oneself
with little, in patience shutting oneself up in hope
in God, resisting the four evil elements and taking
in God's four elements, which are love, meekness,
mercy, and patience in hope. These should man
awaken in himself, and therewith continually fight
against the devil's four elements.

23. Man must here be at war against himself, if
he wishes to become a heavenly citizen. He must

not be a lazy sleeper, and with gormandizing and swilling fill his belly, whereby the devil's elements begin to qualify; but he must be temperate, sober and vigilant, as a soldier that stands before his enemy. For God's wrath fights continually against him; he will have enough to do to defend himself.

24. For the devil is his enemy, his own corrupt flesh and blood is his enemy, God's wrath is his enemy within him, and the whole world is his enemy. Wherever he looks he sees enemies, who all desire to rob him.

25. Therefore fighting must be the watchword, not with tongue and sword, but with mind and spirit; and not give over. Though body and soul should break, yet God must remain the strength of the heart, as David says (Psal. lxxiii. 26). And though a man should see that the whole world were godless, if he purpose becoming a child of God, he must nevertheless continue steadfast.

26. And though it should seem to him that he were alone in this path, and the whole world should say: Thou art a fool, and art mad! yet he should be as if he were dead in the world, and heard that from the mouth of the devil, who is his worst enemy. He should nowhere give ground; but think that in his purpose he pleases God, and that God himself in him is his purpose; that he would thus deliver him from the devil, and bring him into his kingdom. Amen.

SEX PUNCTA MYSTICA

OR

A SHORT EXPLANATION OF

SIX MYSTICAL POINTS

Written in the year 1620

PREFACE

THE precious knowledge is not found unless the soul have once conquered in the assault and struck down the devil, so that it obtains the knight's garland, which the gracious virgin Chastity puts upon it as a token of victory that it has overcome in its dear champion Christ. Then the wonderful knowledge rises, but with no perfection.

THE FIRST POINT

1. All that is substantial and tangible is in this world. Now, since the soul is not a substance or entity in this world, neither is its blood and water a substance or entity in this world.

2. Certainly the soul with its blood and water is in the outer blood and water; but its substance is magical. For the soul is also a magical fire, and its image or form is generated in the light (in the power of its own fire and light) from the magical fire; and yet is a veritable image in flesh and blood, but in the original state thereof.

3. As God's wisdom has being, and yet it, wisdom, is not a being; so the soul with its image has being, and yet it, the soul, is only a magical fire, but its sustenance is from its substance.

4. As a fire must have substance if it is to burn, so likewise the magical fire of the soul has flesh, blood and water. There would be no blood if the tincture of fire and light were not in water. This tincture is the ens or life of wisdom (which has in it all the forms of Nature), and is the other magical fire.

5. For it gives all colours; and from its form goes forth divine power in the gentle nature of the light (understand, according to the property of the

light in it); and according to the property of the fire in it, it is a sharpness of transmutation. It can bring everything to its highest degree; although it is not a live spirit, but the supreme ens.

6. Hence also the tincture is such an ens in water, and introduces thereinto the property of fire and of light, with all the powers of Nature; whereby it transforms the water into blood; and this it does in the outer and inner water, as in the outer and inner blood.

7. The inner blood of the divine substantiality is also magical; for it is Magic which makes it into substance. It is spiritual blood, which outer nature cannot touch (*rügen*), but by imagination only. The inner imagination introduces the outer will into the inner blood, whereby the flesh and blood of the divine substantiality is corrupted, and the noble image of the likeness of God is eclipsed.

8. The soul's flesh and blood is in the highest mystery, for it is divine substantiality. And when the outer flesh and blood die, it falls unto the outer mystery, and the outer mystery falls unto the inner.

9. And every magical fire has its brightness and darkness in itself; on account of which a final day of separation is appointed, when all must pass through a fire and be proved, what shall be fit for it or not. Then everything goes into its own magic, and thereafter is as it was from eternity.

THE SECOND POINT

1. God is from eternity alone all. His essence divides itself into three eternal distinctions. One is the fire-world, the second the dark world, and the third the light-world. And yet they are but one essence, one in another; but one is not the other.

2. The three distinctions are alike eternal and without bounds, and confined in no time nor place. Each distinction shuts itself in itself in a being; and its qualification is in accordance with its property, and in its qualification is also its desire, as the *centrum naturae*.

3. And the desire is its making, for desire makes being where there is none, and that in the essence of the desire, according to the property of the desire. And all is together only a *Magia*, or a hunger after being.

4. Each form makes being in its desire; and each form fulfils itself out of the mirror of its brightness, and has its seeing in its own mirror. Its seeing is a darkness for another mirror, its form is hidden to another eye; but in feeling there is a difference.

5. For each form derives its feeling from the

original state of the first three forms in Nature, viz. from sour, bitter and anguish; and yet in these three there is no pain in themselves, but fire causes pain in them, and light transforms it into gentleness again.

6. The right life is rooted in fire; there is the hinge of light and darkness. The hinge is desire; with whatever it fill itself, to the fire thereof the desire belongs, and its light shines from that fire. That light is the form or seeing of that life; and the substance introduced in the desire is the fire's wood, from which the fire burns, be it harsh or soft; and that also is its kingdom of heaven or of hell.

7. Human life is the hinge between light and darkness; to whichever it give itself up, in that same does it burn. If it give itself to the desire of essence, it burns in anguish, in the fire of darkness.

8. But if it give itself to a nothing, then it is desireless, and falls unto the fire of light, and then it cannot burn in any pain; for it brings into its fire no substance from which a fire could burn. Seeing then there is no pain in it, neither can the life receive any pain, for there is none in it; it has fallen unto the first *Magia*, which is God in his triad.

9. When the life is born, it has all the three worlds in it. The world to which it unites itself, by that it is held, and in that fire enkindled.

10. For when the life enkindles itself, it is attracted by all the three worlds; and they are in motion in the essence, as in the first enkindled fire.

Whatever essence the life in its desire takes in and receives, its fire burns.

11. If the first essence in which the life enkindles itself be good, then is also the fire pleasant and good. But if it be evil and dark, consisting of a fierce wrathful property, then is the fire also a wrath-fire, and has a corresponding desire conforming to the property of the fire.

12. For every imagination desires only essence like unto itself, wherein it originally arose.

13. The life of man in this time is like a wheel, where the undermost is soon uppermost. It enkindles itself at every essence, and soils itself with every essence. But its bath is the movement of the heart of God, a water of gentleness; and therefrom it is able to introduce substantiality into its fire-life. The election of God depends not on the first essence.

14. For the first essence is only the mysterium for a life; and the first life with the enkindling belongs properly to its mysterium out of which it proceeded, be it a wholly fierce essence, or a mixed essence, or an essence of light according to the light-world.

15. The property from which the life first takes its rise, from that also burns the light of its life. This life has no election, and no judgment is passed upon it; for it stands in its own primitive condition, and carries its judgment in itself. It separates itself from all other source (*Qual*); for it burns only in its own source, in its own magical fire.

16. Election is in respect of that which is introduced, whether it belong to the light or to the

darkness.   For according as it belongs to the one property or to the other, so also is its life's will. And here it becomes known whether it is of the fierce wrathful essence, or of the love-essence. So long as it burns in one fire, it is forsaken of the other; and the election of that fire wherein it burns passes upon the life ; for it would have it, it is of its property.

17. But if that fire's will (as the flying *punctum*) plunge into another fire and enkindle itself therein, then it may enkindle the whole life with that fire, if it remain in that fire.

18. Then is the life new-born, either unto the dark world or unto the world of light (in whichever the will has enkindled itself), and upon it comes another election.   And that is the reason why God suffers people to teach, and so does the devil.   Each wishes the life's will to plunge into his fire, and enkindle itself.   And then one mysterium seizes the other.

THE THIRD POINT

ON SIN. WHAT IS SIN, AND HOW IT IS SIN.[1]

1. A thing that is one has neither commandment nor law. But if it mix with another, then there are two beings in one, and also two wills, one running counter to the other. There is the origin of enmity.

2. Thus we are to consider of enmity against God. God is one and good, without any pain or limiting characteristic (*Qual*); and though all source or quality (*Qual*) be in him, yet it is not manifest. For the good has swallowed up the evil or contrary into itself, and keeps it in restraint in the good, as it were a prisoner; for the evil must be a cause of life and of light, but immanifest. But the good dies to the evil, that it may dwell in the evil, without pain or feeling, in itself.

3. Love and enmity are only one thing; but each dwells in itself, and that makes two things. Death is the bound of separation between them; and yet there is no death, save that the good dies to the evil, as the light is dead to the pain of fire, and no longer feels the fire.

4. Thus then must we explain sin in human life. For life is one and good; but if there be another quality therein, then it (life) is an enmity

[1] *i.e.* What things are sins, and what makes them sins.

against God; for God dwells in the highest life of man.

5. Now, no unfathomable existence can dwell in one that is fathomable. For, as soon as the right life awakens pain in itself, it is not identical with the unground, in which there is no pain; hence immediately one separates from the other.

6. For the good or the light is as a nothing; but if something come into it, then this something is another than the nothing. For the something dwells in itself, in torment (*Qual*); for where there is something, there must be a quality (*Qual*) which makes and keeps the something.

7. And thus we are to consider of love and enmity. Love has but one quality and one will, it desires only its like, and not many. For the good is only one, but quality is many; and the human will that desires many, brings into itself, into the One (wherein God dwells), the torment of plurality.

8. For the something is dark, and darkens the life's light; and the One is Light, for it loves itself and is no desire after several.

9. The life's will must therefore be directed towards the One (as towards the good), and thus it remains in one quality. But if it imaginate into another quality, it makes itself pregnant with the thing after which it longs.

10. And if this thing be without an eternal foundation, in a frail perishable root, then it seeks a root for its preservation, that it may remain. For every life stands in magical fire; and every fire must have substance in which it burns.

11. This same thing must make for itself sub-

stance according to its desire, that its fire may have food to feed upon. Now, no fire-source can subsist in the free fire; for it attains not that, inasmuch as it is only a self-thing.

12. All that is to subsist in God must be freed from its own will. It must have no individual fire burning in it; but God's fire must be its fire. Its will must be united to God, that God and the will and spirit of man may be but one.

13. For that which is one is not at enmity with itself, for it has only one will. Wherever it goes, or whatever it does, that is all one with it.

14. One will has only one imagination; and the imagination makes or desires only that which assimilates with it. And so in like manner we are to understand concerning the contrary will.

15. God dwells in all things; and nothing comprehends him, unless it be one with him. But if it go out from the One, it goes out of God into itself, and is another than God, which separates itself. And here it is that law arises, that it should proceed again out of itself into the One, or else remain separated from the One.

16. And thus it may be known what is sin, or how it is sin. Namely, when the human will separates itself from God into an existence of its own, and awakens its own self, and burns in its own fire, which is not capable of the divine fire.

17. For all into which the will enters, and will have as its own, is something foreign in the one will of God. For all is God's, and to man's own will belongs nothing. But if it be in God, then all is its also.

18. Thus we recognize that desire is sin. For it is a lusting out of one into many, and introduces many into one. It will possess, and yet should be will-less. By desire substance is sought, and in substance desire kindles fire.

19. Now each particular fire burns in accordance with the character of its own being; and here separation and enmity are born. For Christ says: He that is not with me is against me; and he that gathereth not with me scattereth (Luke xi. 23). For he gathereth without Christ; and whatsoever is not in Him is out of God.

20. We see, then, that covetousness is sin; for it is a desire out of God. And we see also that pride is sin, for it will be a thing of its own; and separates itself from God, as from the One.

21. For whatever will be in God must walk in him, in his will. Seeing then we are in God but one in many members, it is against God when one member withdraws itself from the other, and makes a lord of itself, as pride does. Pride will be lord, and God alone is lord. Thus there are two lords, and one separates from the other.

22. All, therefore, is sin and a contrary will, that desire possesses as its own, be it meat or drink. If the will imagine thereinto, it fills itself therewith and kindles the fire thereof, and then another fire burns in the first, and there is contrary will and error.

23. Therefore out of the contrary will must grow a new will, which gives itself up again to the one Unity; and the contrary will must be broken and slain.

24. And here we are to consider the Word of God that became man. If man place his desire therein, he goes out from pain (*Qual*), from his own fire, and is new-born in the Word. And thus the out-going will dwells in God; and the first will in greed, earthliness and plurality.

25. Accordingly plurality with the body must break, and it (plurality) must perish and fall away from the out-going will, and then the out-going will is recognized as a new birth. For in the One it takes all again into itself; but not with its own desire, but with [1] its own love—a love that is united with God, that God may be all in all, and his will the will of all things; for in God exists but a single will.

26. Thus we find that evil must be subservient unto the life of the good, provided the will again goes out from the evil, from itself, into the good; for fierceness must constitute life's fire.

27. But the life's will must be turned against itself in conflict; for it must flee from fierceness, and not will it. It must not will desire, and yet its fire (*i.e.* life's fire) wills desire, and must have desire Therefore the thing is, to be born anew in will.

28. Every will-spirit that remains in the desire of its life's fire (as in the ferventness of the wood for fire), or enters thereinto and possesses the earthly, is separated from God as long as it possesses what is foreign, viz. the earthly.

[1] Mr. H. H. Joachim writes: 'Böhme's point here is very deep: the individual's will when united with God does not lose its individuality. It takes all into itself with a love *peculiar to itself*—but since it is *love*, and not *desire*, it (the love) can be the will's very own, peculiar to it, and yet not separate it from other individuals or from God.'

29. Thus, we recognize how superfluity of meat and drink produces sin. For the pure will, which goes out from the life's fire, is drowned in desire and imprisoned, so that it proves too powerless in combat. For the source of fire (or of desire) holds it captive and fills it with craving, so that this same will carries its imagination into the desire.

30. Accordingly the will in the desire for meat and drink is earthly, and is separated from God. But the will that escapes from the earthly fire, burns in the inward fire, and is divine.

31. This will that flees from the earthly desire arises not from the earthly fire. No ; it is the will of the soul's fire, which is caught and concealed by the earthly desire. It wills not to remain in the earthly desire, but will enter into its One, into God, out of which it originally sprang.

32. But if it be kept a prisoner in the earthly desire, then it is shut up in death, and suffers agony. And thus is sin to be understood.

THE FOURTH POINT

1. At the creation of the world and of all being, the Father put himself in motion in accordance with his property, viz. by the centre of Nature, by the dark world and the fire-world. These continued in motion and domination till the Father moved himself in accordance with his heart (and the light-world), and God became man. Then the love of the light overcame the Father's fierce wrathful property, and the Father ruled in the Son with love.

2. Then the Son had dominion in those that did cleave unto God; and the Holy Spirit (that proceeds from the Father and Son) drew men in the light of love, through the Son, to God the Father.

3. But in the end the Holy Spirit moves in the Father's and also in the Son's property, and both properties become active at once. The spirit of the Father reveals itself in fire and light, as also in the wrath of the dark world. Then the kingdom falls unto the Father. For the Holy Spirit must govern eternally, and be an eternal revealer in the light-world and also in the dark world.

4. For the two worlds will stand still; and the Holy Spirit who proceeds from the Father and

Son, bears rule eternally in the two worlds, according to each world's nature and property.

5. He alone will be the revealer of the wonders. And thus to the Father (who is all) the eternal dominion, which he exercises with the Spirit, is delivered by the Son.

THE FIFTH POINT

1. Magic is the mother of eternity, of the being of all beings; for it creates itself, and is understood in desire.

2. It is in itself nothing but a will, and this will is the great mystery of all wonders and secrets, but brings itself by the imagination of the desireful hunger into being.

3. It is the original state of Nature. Its desire makes an imagination (*Einbildung*), and imagination or figuration is only the will of desire. But desire makes in the will such a being as the will in itself is.

4. True Magic is not a being, but the desiring spirit of the being. It is a matrix without substance, but manifests itself in the substantial being.

5. Magic is spirit, and being is its body; and yet the two are but one, as body and soul is but one person.

6. Magic is the greatest secrecy, for it is above Nature, and makes Nature after the form of its will. It is the mystery of the Ternary, viz. it is in desire the will striving towards the heart of God.

7. It is the formative power in the eternal wisdom, as a desire in the Ternary, in which the eternal wonder

of the Ternary desires to manifest itself in co-opera-
tion with Nature.   It is the desire which introduces
itself into the dark Nature, and through Nature into
fire, and through fire, through death or fierceness,
into the light of Majesty.

8. It is not Majesty, but the desire in Majesty.
It is the desire of the divine power, not the power
itself, but the hunger or craving in the power.   It is
not God's Almightiness, but the directrix in God's
power and might.   The heart of God is the power,
and the Holy Spirit is the revelation of power.

9. It is, however, the desire not only in the power,
but also in the conducting spirit; for it has in it the
Fiat.   What the Will-spirit reveals in it, that it
brings into a being by the sourness which is the
Fiat; all according to the model of the will.   According as the will makes a model in wisdom, so
does desiring Magic receive it; for it has in its
property imagination as a longing.

10. Imagination is gentle and soft, and resembles
water.   But Desire is harsh and dry, like a hunger;
it makes the soft hard, and is found in all things,
for it is the greatest thing (*Wesen*) in the Deity.   It
leads the bottomless to foundation, and the nothing
into something.

11. In Magic are all forms of Being of all beings.
It is a mother in all three worlds, and makes each
thing after the model of that thing's will.   It is
not the understanding, but it is a creatrix according to the understanding, and lends itself to good
or to evil.

12. All that the will models in wisdom, if the
will of the understanding also enter thereinto, that

does Magic make into a being. It serves those that love God in God's Being; for it makes in the understanding divine substance, and takes this from imagination, as from the gentleness of the light.

13. It is Magic that makes divine flesh; and the understanding is born of wisdom, for it is a discerner of colours, powers and virtues. The understanding guides the right true spirit with a bridle; for the spirit is soaring, and the understanding is its fire.

14. The spirit is not dissentient, that it should dissent from the understanding; but it is the will of the understanding. But the senses in the understanding are flying-out and dissentient.

15. For the senses are the flash from the fire-spirit, and bring with them in the light the flames of Majesty; and in the darkness they bring with them the flash of terror, as a fierce flash of fire.

16. The senses are such a subtle spirit that they enter into all beings, and take up all beings into themselves. But the understanding tries all in its own fire; it rejects the evil and retains the good. Then Magic, its mother, takes this and brings it into a being.

17. Magic is the mother from which Nature comes, and the understanding is the mother coming from Nature. Magic leads into a fierce fire, and the understanding leads its own mother, Magic, out of the fierce fire into its own fire.

18. For the understanding is the fire of power, and Magic the burning fire; and yet it is not to be understood as fire, but the power or mother to

fire. Fire is called the principle, and Magic is called desire.

19. By Magic is everything accomplished, both good and bad. Its own working is *Nigromantia,* but it is distributed into all the properties. In that which is good it is good, and in that which is evil it is evil. It is of use to the children for God's kingdom, and to the sorcerers for the devil's kingdom ; for the understanding can make of it what it pleases. It is without understanding, and yet comprehends all ; for it is the comprehension of all things.

20. It is impossible to express its depth, for it is from eternity a ground and support of all things. It is a master of philosophy, and likewise a mother thereof.

21. But philosophy leads Magic, its mother, as it pleases. As the divine power, viz. the Word (or heart of God), leads the severe Father into gentleness ; so also does philosophy (or the understanding) lead its mother into a gentle divine quality.

22. Magic is the book of all scholars. All that will learn, must first learn Magic, be it a high or a lowly art. Even the peasant in the field must go to the magical school, if he would cultivate his field.

23. Magic is the best theology, for in it true faith is both grounded and found. And he is a fool that reviles it ; for he knows it not, and blasphemes against God and himself, and is more a juggler than a theologian of understanding.

24. As one that fights before a mirror, and

knows not what the quarrel is, for his fighting is superficial; so also the unjust theologian looks on Magic through a reflection, and understands nothing of the power. For it is godlike, and he is ungodlike, yea devilish, according to the property of each principle. In sum : Magic is the activity in the Will-spirit.

THE SIXTH POINT

1. Mystery is nothing else than the magical will, which still lies caught in desire. It may fashion itself in the mirror of wisdom how it will. And as it fashions itself in the tincture, so it is fixed and formed in Magic, and brought into a being.

2. For *Mysterium magnum* is nothing else than the hiddenness of the Deity, together with the Being of all beings, from which one mysterium proceeds after another, and each mysterium is the mirror and model of the other. And it is the great wonder of eternity, wherein all is included, and from eternity has been seen in the mirror of wisdom. And nothing comes to pass that has not from eternity been known in the mirror of wisdom.

3. But you must understand this according to the properties of the mirror, according to all the forms of Nature, viz. according to light and darkness, according to comprehensibility and incomprehensibility, according to love and wrath, or according to fire and light, as has been set forth elsewhere.

4. The Magician has power in this Mystery to act according to his will, and can do what he pleases.

5. But he must be armed in that element wherein he would create; else he will be cast out as a stranger, and given into the power of the spirits thereof, to deal with him according to their desire. Of which in this place no more is to be said, because of the *turba*.

MYSTERIUM PANSOPHICUM

OR

A FUNDAMENTAL STATEMENT

CONCERNING THE

EARTHLY AND HEAVENLY MYSTERY

HOW THEY ARE IN ONE ANOTHER, AND HOW IN
THE EARTHLY THE HEAVENLY IS MANIFESTED

DRAWN UP IN NINE TEXTS

WHERE BABEL, THE GREAT CITY ON EARTH, IS
TO BE SEEN WITH ITS POWER AND MARVELS. WHY
BABEL IS BORN, AND FROM WHAT. WHERE
ANTICHRIST SHALL STAND NAKED

A most wonderful revelation, taken out of the highest arcanum. Herein is wholly revealed what the *turba* of all beings is.

Written for the children of God, who by such warning will flee from burning Babel, and shall be born children of God out of the *turba*.

All very earnestly and faithfully given from knowledge of the great Mystery, the 8th May, 1620

THE FIRST TEXT

THE unground is an eternal nothing, but makes
an eternal beginning as a craving. For the nothing
is a craving after something. But as there is
nothing that can give anything, accordingly the
craving itself is the giving of it, which yet also is
a nothing, or merely a desirous seeking. And
that is the eternal origin of Magic, which makes
within itself where there is nothing; which makes
something out of nothing, and that in itself only,
though this craving is also a nothing, that is,
merely a will. It has nothing, and there is
nothing that can give it anything; neither has it
any place where it can find or repose itself.

THE SECOND TEXT

1. Seeing then there is a craving in the nothing, it makes in itself the will to something. This will is a spirit, as a thought, which goes out of the craving and is the seeker of the craving, for it finds its mother or the craving. Then is this will a Magician in its mother; for it has found in the nothing something, viz. its mother, and so now it has a place for its dwelling.

2. And herein understand that the will is a spirit, and different from the desirous craving. For the will is an insensitive and incognitive life; but the craving is found by the will, and is in the will a being. Thus the craving is a *Magia*, and the will a *Magus*; and the will is greater than its mother which gives it, for it is lord in the mother; and the mother is dumb, but the will is a life without origin. The craving is certainly a cause of the will, but without knowledge or understanding. The will is the understanding of the craving.

3. Thus we give you in brief to consider of nature and the spirit of nature, what there has been from eternity without origin. And we find thus that the will, viz. the spirit, has no place for its rest; but the craving is its own place, and the will is a band to it, and yet is not held in check.

THE THIRD TEXT

1. Seeing then the eternal will is free from the craving, but the craving is not free from the will (for the will rules over the craving), we recognize the will as the eternal Omnipotence. For it has no parallel. The craving is indeed a movement of attraction or desire, but without understanding; it has a life, but without knowledge.

2. Now the will governs the life of the craving, and doth therewith what it will. And though it doth somewhat, yet this is not known till the same reveals itself through the will, so that it becomes an entity in the life of the will; then it is known what the will has wrought.

3. We recognize, therefore, the eternal Will-spirit as God, and the moving life of the craving as Nature. For there is nothing prior, and either is without beginning, and each is a cause of the other, and an eternal bond.

4. Thus the Will-spirit is an eternal knowing of the unground, and the life of the craving an eternal being [body] of the will.

THE FOURTH TEXT

1. Seeing then the craving is a process of desire, and this desire a life, this same desiring life goes in the craving forward, and is always pregnant with the craving.

2. And the desire is a stern attraction, and yet hath nothing but itself, or the eternity without foundation. And it draws magically, viz. its own desiring into a substance.

3. For the will takes where there is nothing. It is a lord and possessor. It is itself not a being, and yet rules in being, and being makes it desirous, namely of being. And since it becomes in itself desirous, it is magical, and makes itself pregnant, viz. by spirit without being; for originally it is only spirit. Thus it makes in its imagination only spirit, and becomes pregnant with spirit as with the eternal knowing of the unground, in the All-power of the life, without being.

4. As then it is pregnant, the engenderment goes within itself, and dwells in itself. For the essence of the other life cannot grasp this pregnation, and be its container. Hence the pregnation must go within itself and be its own container, as a Son in the eternal Spirit.

5. And as this pregnation has no being, then that is a voice or sound, as a Word of the spirit;

and yet remains in the primitive condition of spirit,
for it hath else no seat.

6. But in this Word is a will, which desires to
go out into a being. This will is the life of the
original will, and proceeds out of the pregnation,
as out of the mouth of the will, into the life of
Magic, viz. into Nature; and reveals the non-
understanding life of Magic, so that the same is
a mysterium in which an understanding exists
essentially, and thus obtains an essential spirit.
There, every essence is an arcanum or a mysterium
of an entire being, and is thus a comprehension as
an unfathomable wonder of eternity; for many
lives without number are generated, and yet all
is together but one being.

7. The threefold Spirit without being is its master
and possessor; and yet it possesses not the Nature-
being, for it (the Spirit) dwells in itself.

8. The Word is its centre or seat, and is in the
midst as a heart; and the spirit of the Word, which
takes its origin in the primal eternal will, reveals
the wonders of the essential life. There are, then,
two mysteries: one in the spirit-life, and one in
the essential life. The spirit-life is acknowledged
as God, and is rightly so called; and the essential
life is acknowledged as the Nature-life, which would
have no understanding if the Spirit or the spirit-
life were not desirous. In this desire the divine
Being, as the eternal word or heart of God, is
continually and from eternity generated; from
which the desiring will as Spirit eternally goes out
into the Nature-life, and reveals therein the
mystery in essences. So that there are two lives

and also two beings, from and in a single, eternal, unfathomable origin.

9. And thus we apprehend what God and Nature is; how the one and the other is from eternity without any ground or beginning. For it is an everlasting beginning. It begins itself perpetually and from eternity to eternity, where there is no number; for it is the unground.

THE FIFTH TEXT

1. Seeing then there have been from eternity two beings, we cannot say that one exists beside the other, and is disposed so that the one comprehends the other; neither can it be said that one is outside of the other, and that there is a separation. No; but thus we apprehend it, that the spirit-life faces inwards, and the nature-life outwards and forwards.

2. Together, then, we compare them to a spherical orb which goeth on all sides, as the wheel in Ezekiel indicates.

3. The spirit-life is an entire fulness of the nature-life, and yet is not laid hold of by the nature-life. They are two principles in a single origin, each having its mystery and its operation. The nature-life works unto fire, and the spirit-life unto the light of glory. By fire we understand the fierceness of the consuming of the essentiality of Nature; and by light the production of water, which deprives the fire of power, as is set forth in the *Forty Questions on the soul*.

4. And thus we are able to recognize an eternal substantiality of Nature, identical with water and fire, which are as it were mixed together; where then this gives a light-blue colour, like the flash of fire; where it hath a form as a ruby mixed with crystal

in one substance, or as yellow, white, red and blue mingled in a dark water; where it is as blue in green, yet each has its lustre, and shines. And the water checks the fire, so that there is no consuming there, but an eternal essence or substance in two mysteries united in one another, and yet the distinction of two principles as two kinds of life.

5. And thus we understand here the essence of all beings, and that it is a magical essence, as a will can create itself in the essential life, and so enter into a birth, and in the great Mystery, in the origin of fire, awaken a source which before was not manifest, but lay hidden in mystery like a gleam in the multiplicity of colours; as we have a mirror of this in the devils and in all malignity. And we recognize also from whence all things, evil and good, take their origin, namely from the Imagination in the great Mystery, where a wonderful essential life generates itself.

6. As we have a sufficient knowledge thereof by the creatures of this world, as where the divine Life awakened once for all the Nature-life, when it brought forth such wonderful creatures from the essential mystery; whereby we understand that every essence is come to be a mysterium or a life, and also that in the great Mystery there is a magical craving, so that the craving of every essence makes in its turn a mirror, to see and to know itself in the mirror.

7. And then the craving seizes this (namely the mirror), brings it into its imagination, and finds that it is not of its life. Hence opposition arises and loathing, so that the craving would

discard the mirror, and yet cannot. And therefore the craving seeks the limit of the beginning, and passes out of the mirror. Thus the mirror is broken, and the breaking is a *turba*, as a dying of the formed or comprehended life.

8. And it is highly recognizable by us how the imagination of the Eternal Nature has the *turba* in the craving, in the Mystery, but not awakenable, unless the creature, as the mirror of eternity, doth itself awaken this, viz. the fierce wrath, which in eternity is hidden in mystery.

9. And we see here, when the Eternal Nature put itself in motion once for all by the creation of the world, that the fierce wrath was awakened too, and also manifested itself in creatures. As indeed we find many evil beasts, likewise herbs and trees, as also worms, toads, serpents and the like,—of which the Eternal Nature hath a loathing, and the malignity and poison is nourished only in its own essence.

10. And therefore the Eternal Nature seeks the limit of the malignity, and would abandon it. Then it falls into the *turba*, as into a dying; and yet there is no dying, but a spewing-out in the Mystery, where the malignity with its life must stand apart as in a darkness. For the Eternal Nature abandons it and casts it into shade, so that it stands thus by itself as an evil, poisonous, fierce mysterium, and is itself its own magic as a craving of the poisonful anguish.

THE SIXTH TEXT

1. When we consider and take cognizance of ourselves, we find the opposition of all essences, each being the loathing of the other, and enemy to the other.

2. For every will desires a purity without *turba* in the other essence; and yet has itself the *turba* in it, and is also the loathing of the other. Then the power of the greater extends over the lesser and holds it in subjection, unless it escape from it; otherwise the strong rules over the weak. Therefore the weak doth run, and seeks the limit of the driver or oppressor, and would be free from compulsion. And thus the limit, which is hidden in mystery, is sought by all creatures.

3. And hence arises all the power of this world, that one rules over the other. And this was not in the beginning commanded or ordained by the highest good, but grew out of the *turba*. Afterward Nature acknowledged it as her own being, which was born from her, and gave it laws, to generate itself further in the framed government. Where then this birth has climbed to regal prerogative, and has moreover sought the abyss, as the One, till it is become monarchy or

empire. And there it is climbing still, and will be one and not many. And though it be in many, yet will the first source, from which all is generated, rule over all, and will alone be a lord over all governments.

4. And as this craving was in the beginning one government, but in time divided itself into many according to the essences; therefore the plurality again seeks the One, and it is certainly born in the sixth number of the crown, in the six thousandth year in the figure; not at the end, but in the hour of the day in which the creation of the wonders was completed.

5. That is, when the wonders of the *turba* are in the end, a Lord is born who governs the whole world, but by many forms of administration.

6. And then the self-grown authority and the oppressor will be sought; for the lesser, who hath lain under, has run to the limit. Then everything separates itself, for it is at the limit, and there is no staying or revoking.

7. Also the *turba*, as the fierce wrath of all creatures, will be sought; for it has with the loathing of the creatures run to the limit, and now becomes manifest, viz. in the midst, in the number of the crown, in the six thousandth year, a little over, not under.

8. In the day and the hour when the creation was accomplished in mystery, and was set as a mirror of eternity in the wonders [of this time].[1]

9. That took place on the sixth day, past

[1] The explanatory additions within brackets [ ] are from Claassen's book of extracts.

noon. There [also in the end] the mystery with the wonders is revealed and is known. Where then purity shall drive out the *turba* for a time, till the beginning pass into the end. And then is the mystery [of creation but] a wonder in figures.

THE SEVENTH TEXT

1. Now, seeing in the mystery of the Eternal Nature we have such an arcanum from which all creatures evil and good were generated and created, we recognize it to be a magical essence or substance, where one Magic has by desire awakened another and brought it into being, where everything has elevated itself and carried itself to the highest power. For the Spirit of God is not a maker in Nature, but a revealer and a seeker of the good.

2. Thus hath evil as by magical craving always sought and found itself in the Mystery, and has been revealed apart from the divine purpose. For fierceness is a harsh rigorousness, and rules over the simple.

3. All has, therefore, grown from its own tree without premeditation. For the first revealer, viz. God, ordained not malignity to the government, but reason or wit, which was to reveal the wonders and be a guide of life. And here there meets us the great secret which has from eternity existed in mystery, viz. the Mystery with its colours, which are four. The fifth is not proper to the mysterium of Nature, but is of the Mysterium of God, and shines in the mysterium of Nature as a living light.

4. And these are the colours wherein all things lie : blue, red, green and yellow. The fifth, white, belongs to God ; and yet has also its lustre in Nature. It is the fifth essence, a pure unblemished child ; as is to be seen in gold and silver, and in a white clear stone that resists fire.

5. For fire is the proof or trial of all the colours, in which none subsists but white, the same being a reflection of God's Majesty. The black colour belongs not to the mystery [of the wonders of creation], but is the veil or the darkness wherein all things lie.

6. Further, we find here the tree of tongues or languages, with four alphabets. One signed with the characters of the Mystery, in which is found the language of Nature, which in all languages is the root. But in the birth of plurality (or of many languages) it is not known save by its own children, to whom the Mystery itself gives understanding ; for it is a wonder of God. This alphabet of the language of Nature is hidden among them all in the black colour ; for the black colour belongs not to the number of colours. The same is mystery and not understood, save by him who possesses the language of Nature, to whom it is revealed by God's Spirit.

7. The second alphabet is the Hebrew, which reveals the mystery [of the language of Nature], and names the tree with the branches and twigs.

8. The third is the Greek, which names the tree with the fruit and every ornament, and first correctly expresses knowledge.

9. The fourth is the Latin (to which many nations

and tongues have recourse), which expresses the tree with its power and virtue.

10. The fifth is God's Spirit, which is the revealer of all alphabets ; and this alphabet can no man learn, unless it reveal itself in man's spirit.

11. These alphabets take their origin from the colours of the great Mystery, and distribute themselves moreover into seventy-seven languages ; although we recognize only five for chief languages, and seventy-two for the marvels wherein Babel is understood, as a mouth of a confusedness. There reason abandoned her guide and willed to go alone, and to climb aloft into the Mystery.

12. As is to be known by the children of Nimrod at the tower of Babel, when they had fallen from obedience to God into their own individual reason ; then they had lost their guide and did confound reason, so that they comprehended not their own language.

13. Thus many languages, viz. seventy-two, grew out of confused Babel, and each entered into itself and sought knowledge, each in its own reason and iniquity ; for they had forsaken God and were become heathens. And he suffered them to walk in their wonders, for they would not cleave unto him, but would be a special self-ful growth. And their own reason (which was mixed of all the colours) had to rule them.

14. Then the *turba* was born, so that they were not of one mind ; for every one would live under guidance of his own colour. And yet these were not the true chief colours, but only their evil self-hatched children, who hatched themselves out

in reason.   And they ran without the right guide, who had created all in one tongue, and revealed no more than one,—one tree with the branches and the power together with the fruit.

15. For the four alphabets are in one tree, and proceed from one another.   But the multitude of languages must have recourse to their characters as members of the same family, and yet also will be their very own.   And all shoot forth in opposition to the tree.

THE EIGHTH TEXT

1. We see here the origin of two sorts of religions, from which Babel as an idol-god is born, and that in heathens and Jews.

2. For Babel is in both, and they are two races in one. One, under guidance of its reason (as of the life and spirit of Nature), goes forward and seeks to elevate itself. It makes itself a way in its being; for its will proceeds out of its own craving and seeks its magic, as a great number for its government, and goes simply out of itself forward. Its will remains in its plurality, and is the god and guide of its plurality.

3. And though the Free-will of God oppose it and reprove it, yet the idol-god only flatters with its lips the Free-will, viz. the Spirit of God, and honours its own will in the number of plurality. For this will is generated from its treasure, from its own magic, and comprehends not the Free-will of God. It is born therefore from flesh and blood, from its own nature; and is a child of this world, and regards its treasure as its love. Hence it is a hypocrite and a confused Babel. The number of plurality and its own magic confuse it, in that it goes out from one number into many. This multiplicity is a confused Babel; and its hypo-

critical mouth, with which it gives good words and
solemnly promises much to the Spirit of Unity,
is an antichrist and a liar.　For it speaks in one way
and acts in another.　Its heart is a craving, and
the spirit of its heart has turned itself to the
craving.

4. Thus the Magician of multiplicity is a proud,
arrogant, covetous, malignant devourer, and a
spirit from the desiring plurality ; and is a false
god.　He is not attached to the Free-will of Nature,
which hath the might of wonders at its command,
and he has no understanding in the Divine Mystery,
for he cleaves not with his will to that Spirit.　Else,
if his will were turned towards Freedom, the Spirit
of God would reveal his magical mystery, and
his wonders and works would, with his will, stand
in God.

5. But seeing they go out from themselves, the
beginning seeks the end, and the middle is the
turba.　For it is not in the Free-will of God ;
but it grows from itself, and elevates itself like a
proud tree.

6. And as God is one only in will, one in
the eternal Desire or in the eternal Magic (so
that the craving of the eternal Magic yields itself
up to the eternal Will, and draws therein its
life), then the apostate will is a perjured whore,
for it is a generatress of falsehood, and hangs not
on the Free-will.

7. And here we understand a separation from
God ; a cause of all this being Lucifer, who made
the Magic of Nature subject to false desire.　Thus
two eternal lives are born : one in the will of God,

the other in the will of the devil and of the fierce wrath; and this is Babel with Antichrist on earth.

8. All that goes out from God's will into its own will belongs to Babel. This is seen in Jews and heathens, and in all peoples.

9. The heathen remained in their own magic. But those who from the itch of corruption passed out into the light of Nature because they did not know God, yet have lived in purity,—these were children of the Free-will, and in them has the Spirit of Freedom revealed great wonders in their mystery, as is to be seen by the wisdom they have bequeathed to us.

10. But the others, who have lived only in their own magical will from flesh and blood,—their will was drowned in the *turba*. And the *turba* streamed forth in their will, and gave them a spirit according to the essences of covetousness and fierceness. These have sought only the number of plurality, as dominions and kingdoms.

11. And when the *turba* could not on account of power advance, it grew furious and began hostilities. And from thence war has its origin, viz. from pride and greed of plurality, and belongs with its number to the Mystery of wrath.

12. Thus also were the Jews. God revealed himself to them, but they were attached also to two wills. One part to the commandment, with their will directed into God's will, as the patriarchs and all the pious hopers of Israel. The others performed with their hands the work of the law, and adhered with their will to their poisoned magic, viz. to covetousness, and sought only their numbers of

plurality. Their mouth was a Jew, and their heart a Babylonish whore, a hypocrite and an antichrist, with fair words and a false covetous heart.

13. And in the same way in Christendom and among all peoples the Babylonish whore with Antichrist is established. In one people dwell at once two kingdoms, and are not miscible in the inward spirit so as to become one, like as clay and iron are not miscible. They mix indeed by the body, but their spirits are two kinds (Dan. ii. 43).

14. Whosoever will know Antichrist, let him seek him thus; he will find him in every house. But the worst of all is the crowned whore; and her sponsors at the baptism of whoredom are the brawlers who lead out of the one will of God into many wills, that they may inherit only the number of plurality, and fatten earthly bellies.

15. And the other part of the Free-will of God proceeds with its magical will out of itself into Freedom, viz. into the one ungraspable will of God. These stand turned backward in the magical figure. Their life seeks bread, and goes forward; yet their will is not in the bread, but passes out of itself, out of the craving, into God. These live with the will in God, in one number; these are children of the eternal true Magic. For God's Spirit dwells in their will, and reveals to them the eternal wonders of God; and their life's spirit reveals the wonders of this world.

16. These are free from Babel and Antichrist, even though they should sit in his lap. For the true image of God is in the spirit of the will, which is generated from the soul's spirit.

THE NINTH TEXT

1. Seeing then there are two Magics in one another, there are also two Magicians who lead them, viz. two spirits. One is God's Spirit, and the other the Reason-spirit, in which the devil ensconces himself. In God's Spirit is the love of unity. And man cannot better prove or try himself than by giving serious attention to what his desire and longing impel him : the same he hath for a leader, and its child he is. Nevertheless, he now has power to break and change that will; for he is magical and possesses the power.

2. But there must be real earnestness; for he must subdue the astral spirit which rules in him. To do this, a sober calm life is necessary, with continual abandonment to God's will. For, to subdue the astral influence, no wisdom nor art will avail; but sobriety of life, with continual withdrawal from the influxes. The elements continually introduce the astral craving into his will. Therefore it is not so easy a thing to become a child of God ; it requires great labour, with much travail and suffering.

3. Antichrist indeed may call himself a child of God. But Christ says : They shall not all enter into the kingdom of heaven who say : Lord, Lord, have we not in thy name cast out devils and done mighty works ? But he saith unto them :

Away from me, ye stinking goats, I know you not (Matt. vii. 21–23). Ye have done this by means of false magic, and have never become known in my spirit and will. Ye are in your spiritual figure goats, tyrants, covetous muckworms, proud arrogants, voluptuaries. Ye have carried my name on your tongue, but sacrificed your heart to pleasure, to the itch of the flesh, and are generated in the *turba*. Ye must be proved by fire. And thus to every kingdom its fruit comes home.

4. Therefore, thou brave world, look at thyself in these writings, which the eternal Ground hath set before thee, and meditate on it further and more deeply. Else thou wilt be caught in thy *turba*. There thou shalt with thy substance pass through the fire of God; and whatsoever is a work out of God's will shall remain in the fire.

5. But whatsoever is done in the will of God shall stand to the honour and glory of God, and for the eternal joy of the image of man.

6. Now think what thou doest. For Babel is already in flames, and begins to burn. There is no longer possible any quenching, nor any remedy. She has been recognized as evil; her kingdom goeth to the end. Hallelujah.

THEOSCOPIA

OR

THE HIGHLY PRECIOUS GATE OF THE

DIVINE INTUITION

SHOWING WHAT *MYSTERIUM MAGNUM* IS, AND
HOW ALL IS FROM, THROUGH AND IN GOD;
HOW GOD IS SO NEAR ALL THINGS,
AND FILLS ALL

———

Written in the year 1622

CHAPTER I

What God is ; and how we shall recognize his divine nature in his manifestation.

1. Reason says : I hear much mention made of God, that there is a God who has created all things, also upholds and supports all things ; but I have not yet seen any, nor heard from the lips of any, that hath seen God, or that could tell where God dwells or is, or how he is. For when Reason looks upon the existence of this world, and considers that it fares with the righteous as with the wicked, and how all things are mortal and frail ; also how the righteous man sees no deliverer to release him from the anxiety and adversity of the wicked man, and so must go down with fear in misery to the grave : then it thinks, all things happen by chance ; there is no God who interests himself in the sufferer, seeing he lets him that hopes in him be in misery, and therein go down to the grave ; neither has any been heard of who has returned from corruption, and said he has been with God.

2. Answer. Reason is a natural life, whose ground lies in a temporal beginning and end, and cannot enter into the supernatural ground wherein God is understood. For though Reason thus views itself in this world, and in its viewing

finds no other ground, yet it finds in itself a desire after a higher ground, wherein it might rest.

3. For it understands that it has proceeded from a supernatural ground, and that there must be a God who has brought it into a life and will. And it is terrified in itself at its willing of wickedness, it is ashamed of its own will, and pronounces itself wrong in the willing of evil. Even though it does wrong, yet it accuses itself, and is afraid of a judgment which it sees not. This signifies that the hidden God, who has brought himself into Nature, dwells in it and reproves it for its evil way; and that the same hidden God cannot be of the nature of perceptibility, since Reason sees not nor comprehends him.

4. On the other hand, forsaken Reason, which here wrongfully (to its thinking) is tormented in misery, finds a desire within it, itself still more to forsake, and willingly gives itself up to suffering. But in its suffering wrong it enters into a hope that that which has created it will take it from suffering into itself; and it desires to rest in that which is not passive, and seeks rest in that which it is not in itself. It desires the death of its egoism, and yet desires not to be a nothing; but desires only to die to suffering (*Qual*), in order that it may rest in itself.

5. It gives itself up therefore to suffering, that the power of pain should kill its suffering, and that it might in its life, through the death of the dying of its Self, in that it is a painful life, enter into the unpainful and unsuffering.

6. Herein we understand rightly the hidden God,

how he reveals himself in the heart of man, and reproves wrong in the conscience, and draws that which suffers wrong by suffering to himself. And how the life of Reason, viz. the natural life, must in suffering get a desire to return again into that out of which it proceeded ; and how it must desire to hate itself, and to die to the natural will, in order that it may attain the supernatural.

7. Reason says : Why has God created a painful, suffering life ? Might it not be in a better state without suffering or pain, seeing he is the ground and beginning of all things ? Why does he permit the contrary will ? Why does he not destroy evil, that only a good may be in all things ?

8. Answer. Nothing without contrariety can become manifest to itself ; for if it has nothing to resist it, it goes continually of itself outwards, and returns not again into itself. But if it return not again into itself, as into that out of which it originally went, it knows nothing of its primal being.[1]

9. If the natural life had no contrariety, and were without a limit, it would never inquire after its ground from which it arose ; and hence the hidden God would remain unknown to the natural life. Moreover, were there no contrariety in life, there would be no sensibility, nor will, nor efficacy therein, also neither understanding nor science. For a thing that has only one will has no divisibility. If it find not a contrary will, which gives occasion to it exercising motion, it stands still. A single thing can know nothing more than a one ; and even though it is in itself good, yet it knows neither

---

[1] Dr. Stirling's rendering of *Urstand*.

evil nor good, for it has nothing in itself to make this perceptible.

10. And so then we can philosophize concerning the will of God, and say: If the hidden God, who is a single existence and will, had not by his will brought himself out of himself, out of the eternal wisdom in the temperament, into divisibility of will, and had not introduced this same divisibility into an inclusiveness for a natural and creaturely life, and had this possibility of separation in life not found expression in strife; how could then the hidden will of God, which in itself is one only, be revealed to himself? How can there be in a single will a knowledge of itself?

11. But if there be a divisibility in the one will, so that the divisibility disposes itself into *centra* and self-will, so that thus in that which is separated there is a will of its own, and thus in a single will unfathomable and innumerable wills arise, like branches from a tree; then we see and understand that in such a divisibility each separated will brings itself into a special form, and that the conflict of the wills is about the form, so that one form in the partibility is not as another, and yet all have their subsistence in one ground.

12. For a single will cannot break itself asunder in pieces, just as the soul (*Gemüth*) breaks not in pieces when it separates into an evil and good willing; but the out-going of sense only separates into a willing of evil and of good, and the soul remains in itself entire, and suffers an evil and good willing to arise and dwell in it.

13. Now saith Reason: Whereto is this good or

useful, that with the good there must be an evil ? Answer. That which is evil or of contrary will occasions the good or the will to press back towards its primal existence, as towards God, and the good, viz. the good will, to become desirous. For a thing that in itself is only good, and has no suffering (*Qual*), desires nothing ; for it knows nothing better in itself or for itself after which it could long.

14. Thus then we can philosophize concerning the one good will of God, and say, that he can desire nothing in himself, for he has nothing in or for himself which could give him anything. And therefore he brings himself out of himself into a divisibility, into *centra*, in order that a contrariety may arise in the emanation, viz. in that which has emanated, that the good may in the evil become perceptible, effectual, and capable of will ; namely to will to separate itself from the evil, and to re-will to enter into the one will of God.

15. But seeing the emanation of the one eternal will of God continually proceeds from himself to his manifestation, the good likewise, as the divine power, flows from the eternal One with this emanation, and enters also into the divisibility and into the *centra* of plurality.

16. Now, the perpetual emanation of the will occasions the good by its motion to long for stand-still again, and to become desirous to repenetrate into the eternal One ; and in such penetration into itself the One becomes mobile and desireful ; and in such working lies feeling, cognition and will.

17. God, so far as he is called God, can will

nothing but himself; for he has nothing before or after him that he can will. But if he will anything, that very same has emanated from him, and is a counterstroke of himself, wherein the eternal will wills in its something. Now if the something were only a one, the will could have no exercise therein. And therefore the unfathomable will has separated itself into beginnings and carried itself into being, that it might work in something, as we have a similitude in the soul (*Gemüth*) of man.

18. If the soul did not itself flow from itself, it would have no sense-perception; but if it had no sense-perception, neither would it have any knowledge of itself, nor of any other thing, and were incapable of doing or working. But the efflux of sense from the soul (which efflux is a counterstroke of the soul, in which the soul feels itself) endows the soul with will or desire, so that it introduces the senses into a something, viz. into a *centrum* of an ego-hood, wherein the soul works through sense, and reveals and contemplates itself in its working through the senses.

19. Now if in these *centra* of sense in the counterstroke of the soul there were no *contrarium*, then all the *centra* of emanated sense were but a one; in all the *centra* of sense but one single will, that did continually but one and the same thing. How could then the wonders and powers of the divine wisdom become known by the soul (which is an image of divine revelation) and be brought into figures?

20. But if there be a *contrarium*, as light and darkness, therein, then this *contrarium* is contrary

to itself, and each quality occasions the other to bring itself into desire to will to fight against the other, and to dominate it.   In which desire, sense and the soul is brought into a natural and creaturely ground to a will of its own, viz. to a domination in its something, or by its *centrum* over all the *centra*, as one sense of the soul over another.

21. Hence struggle and anxiety, also contrary will, take their rise in the soul, so that the whole soul is thereby instigated to enter into a breaking of the senses, and of the self-will of the senses, as of the natural *centra*, and, passing out of the pain of rebellion and strife, out of anxiety, to desire to sink into the eternal rest, as into God, from whence it sprang.

22. And therefrom arise faith and hope, so that the anxious soul hopes for a deliverance, and longs to return to its origin again, viz. to God.

23. So have we likewise to understand the divine manifestation.   For all things have their first beginning from the emanation of the divine will, whether evil or good, love or sorrow ;   and yet the will of God is not a thing, neither nature nor creation, wherein is no pain, sorrow nor contrary will. But from the efflux of the Word, as by the outgoing of the unfathomable mind (which is the wisdom of God or the great Mystery, where the eternal understanding is in the temperament), has flowed understanding and knowledge ;   and this efflux is a beginning of will, when the understanding has separated itself into form.   Thus the forms, each in itself, became desirous to have also a counter-stroke to its similarity.   And this desire is a com-

prehendingness for selfhood or ownness, as for a place, for a something. And through this something the *Mysterium magnum*, as the unnatural power, is become substantial and natural; and the something has comprehended itself so as to become an individual will.

24. For this individual will is a ground of its selfhood, and shuts itself in as a desiring will, whence the magnetic impression for sharpness and hardness has taken its origin; and is a ground of darkness and of painful feeling, whence contrary will, anxiety and flight (sensibility) have their origin; and is a ground of Nature, from whence comes the plurality of the qualities, so that in such a contrariety each will has arisen from the other, to separate itself from pain, like as sense takes its rise from the soul, the soul through the senses being in continual anxiety, working, willing and breaking.

25. In this divine emanation, in which the divine power breathes forth itself from itself, and brings and has brought itself into Nature and creation, we are to recognize two things. First, the eternal understanding of the one good will, which is a temperament, and thus only introduces itself into a sensibility and activity for the manifestation of power, colours and virtue; that power and virtue may be realized in separability, in form, and the eternal wisdom be revealed and pass into knowledge. From thence also the angelic, soulic and creaturely ground has proceeded, as well as thrones and dominions, together with the visible world.

26. And then, secondly, we are to understand the original will of Nature, viz. the comprehensibility of the *centra*, where each *centrum* in the divisibility shuts itself in a place to egoism and self-will as an individual mysterium or mind. Out of which springs unlikeness of will, showing how in these two a *contrarium* arises, for they are two in one.

27. Namely (1) that which is inward from the origin of the divine power requires only a counterstroke to its similarity, viz. something that is good, wherein the good, divine, emanated will may work and manifest itself. Then (2) the self-generated, individual, natural will in the place of the self-hood of the dark impression of the sharpness also requires a likeness, viz. a counterstroke through its own comprehensibility; through which comprehension it makes itself material, and requires nothing but its corporality as a natural ground.

28. In these two we are to understand the good and evil will in all things. And it is herein rightly understood how the inward, spiritual ground of all beings arises from the divine power, and how in all things also an individual, natural desire arises; and how all the bodies of visible, sentient beings have their origin from the desire of Nature.

29. Further, we should clearly observe that just as the individual, natural desire, which has a beginning, makes itself material and makes for itself a counterstroke, viz. a likeness, wherein it works; so also the divine ground and will through the comprehensibility of its love makes for itself a counterstroke and spiritual being, wherein

the divine will works, and introduces the divine
power into forms and separability for the manifestation of the divine power and glory.

30. And in this world always two natures in
one are to be understood : First, an eternal,
divine and spiritual ; and secondly, one that
has a beginning, and is natural, temporal and
perishable in self-will. For two kinds of will
are found in one life : First, one that has a
beginning and is natural, in which the will is an
individual *astrum*, and inqualifies with all that
is external, natural, elemental and sidereal ; and
secondly, an eternal spiritual will, or eternal
spiritual nature, which is a comprehension or comprehended existence of the divine will, with which
the divine will also makes for itself a counterstroke and being, wherein it works. And these
two are understood in two principles : the first
divine in a heavenly, and the second temporal in
an earthly.

31. And as the heavenly hangs on the earthly,
so also does the earthly on the heavenly, and yet
neither is the other. For the heavenly has a
spiritual nature, which is wholly an essential power,
and permeates and pervades the earthly, and yet
possesses only its principle. And it gives power
to the earthly, so that it obtains another new will,
and longs after the heavenly. Which longing is a
desire to go out from the vanity of Nature, whereof
the Scripture says : All creatures do earnestly long
with us to be freed from the vanity to which they
are subjected against their will (Rom. viii. 19–22).

32. Understand it aright. The egressed Desire

of the divine power for Nature, from which Nature and self-will has arisen, longs to be freed from the natural individual will.

33. This Desire is laden with the impression of Nature against its will, for that God has introduced it thereinto. It shall at the end of this time be released from the loaded vanity of Nature, and be brought into a crystalline, clear Nature. Then will be evident why God has shut it up in a time, and subjected it to pain [in the disposition] for suffering : Namely, that through the natural pain the eternal power might be brought into forms, shape and separability for perceptibility; and that creatures, viz. a creaturely life, might be revealed therein in this time, and so be a play in the counterstroke to the divine wisdom. For through folly wisdom becomes manifest, because folly attributes power to its own self, and yet rests upon a [another] foundation and beginning, and has an end.

34. Thus the endless life is displayed to view through folly, in order that therein a praise might arise to the honour of God, and that the eternal and permanent might become known in the mortal.

35. And thus the first question put by Reason is answered, in that it supposes all things happen by chance, and that there is no God, seeing he suffers the righteous man to be in pain, fear and tribulation, and brings him at last to the grave, like the wicked man; so that it seems as if God interested himself in nothing, or as if there were no God, since Reason sees not, knows nor

feels him. Therefore it is declared to it, that it (Reason) is in its own life only a counterstroke to the right life ; and if it find in itself no hunger or desire after that from which in the beginning it arose, that it is in its own life only a foolishness and play, wherein wisdom brings its wonders to pass.

36. For Reason sees in the wise man also such a folly according to the outward nature, and sees how God abandons this folly of the wise, that it must stand in shame and reproach before the self-willed, foolish subtlety, which nevertheless knows not its end. Therefore foolish Reason supposes there is no deliverer, and knows not how the wise man is delivered in himself and freed from the inherited folly by immergence of his own will. For his own will, through the pain and opposition of the godless, enters into its breaking and into its willing nothing, and sinks again into its first origin, as into God's will, and therein is born anew. And that God is not served by the coarse, mortal flesh, that he should introduce deliverance into the animal, self-willed life ; but that to him the matter lies in this, that self-will should break, and sink again into God. Thus is the inward good nature comprehended in God's will; and on the mortal body is the more pain laid, that the individual, natural will may not enter again into a desire of its own for selfhood, and set itself up as a ruler over the inward ground, and destroy the true image of God.

37. This, earthly Reason understands not ; for it knows not how God dwells in it, and what God's

will and nature is. It knows not that God dwells through it, and is so near it ; and that its life is but a foolishness of wisdom, by means of which life wisdom manifests itself, that it may be known what wisdom is. Its will is gone from God into selfhood, and boasts itself of its own power, and sees not how its power has beginning and end, that it is but a play, by which mirror (play) wisdom beholds itself for a time in the folly of the wise ; and, finally, through such pain of the godless, folly in the case of the wise breaks to pieces, in that they begin to hate the frail, foolish life, and to die with Reason, and to give up the will to God.

38. This, earthly Reason regards as a folly, especially when it sees that God also in the wise abandons their earthly folly, and lets the body of such folly, wherein the folly beheld itself, go down without help to the grave. Therefore it supposes this man has received no deliverance from God : Seeing he trusted in Him, his faith must certainly have been false, else He had surely delivered him in his lifetime.

39. Moreover, because it feels not its punishment immediately, it supposes there is no longer possible any serious earnest here ; and knows not that the longer the more it comprehends itself in folly, and becomes in itself a strong source of eternal pain. So that, when for it the light of outer Nature perishes, wherein for a time it has strutted in selfhood, it then stands by itself in darkness and pain, so that its false, own desire is a mere rough, stinging, hard sharpness and contrary will.

40. It hopes during this time in an external

help, and brings itself into pleasure of its will, and holds that for its kingdom of heaven. But when for it the outer light is extinguished in death, it then stands in eternal despair, and neither sees any deliverer about nor within it.

41. But the wise man becomes in this time to himself a fool, and learns to hate his folly (which folly Reason regards as prudence). Accordingly his wisdom (which the world regards as folly) must be a foolishness to Reason, at which it is scandalized. And so also God in the wise man hates the foolish mortal life, just as the wise man hates it himself, in order that the true divine life may rule in him with the understanding. And therefore with God there is no regret for the mortal body of the wise man; for he comprehends his divine Ens in him in his spirit and will, and lets the body of folly with the foolish descend into its grave, till the day of the separation of all beings.

42. And Reason understands not this; therefore it is foolish. And a man should be a man, not according to folly, but according to God's Spirit; and judge what is divine, not according to image-like [creaturely] Reason, for it is written: He that builds on the flesh (viz. on the mortal Reason of his own will) shall of the flesh inherit corruption; but he that builds on the spirit (viz. on the divine will), and places his will in the hope of the divine promise, shall of the spirit inherit eternal life (Gal. vi. 8).

CHAPTER II

*Of the mind, will, and thoughts of human life. How
it has its origin from the will of God, and how
it is an object or an image of God, in which
God wills, works, and dwells.*

1. Reason says : As the mind with the senses
is a natural life with a beginning, which stands
in a time and fragility ; how may it then in this
time be brought to the supersensible divine life ?
Or, how is the divine indwelling in life ?

2. Answer. The life of man is a form of the
divine will, and came from the divine inbreathing
into the created image of man. It is the formed
Word of the divine knowledge ; but has been
poisoned by the counter-breathing of the devil,
and of the fierce wrath of temporal Nature ;
so that the life's will has fashioned itself with
the outward, earthly counterstroke of the mortal
nature, and has come out of its temperament into
separation of qualities.

3. For these reasons it is found still in the earthly
image, and is now to be considered in three principles. In the first Principle, by its true primal
existence, it stands in the outgoing will of God,
in the divine knowledge, which originally was a
temperament, in which the divine power did work

by sense. And therein is rightly understood a paradise or working of divine powers, as a perpetual formation of divine will. And by this budding is to be understood the outgoing of the good senses, whereby the divine wisdom formed itself in figure in a divine manner, and by such formation the divine understanding manifested itself through the outgoing of the life of sense. Hence it was rightly called an image of God, in which the divine will revealed itself.

4. But when this life in the first principle was breathed upon in its image by the fierce wrathful devil, so that the devil whispered it, that it were good and profitable for it that the outgoing of the senses from the life should break itself off from the temperament, and should bring itself into an image of its own according to the properties of plurality, to prove dissimilarity, viz. to know and to be sensible of evil and good;

5. Then the life's own will consented, and brought the senses as the outgoing Desire thereinto; it has introduced itself into desire for ownness, and impressed or comprehended itself in selfhood.

6. And then immediately the life's understanding became manifest in [separated] qualities; Nature has taken the life captive in dissimilarity, and set up her rule. Whence the life is become painful, and the inward divine ground of the good will and nature has been extinguished, that is, has become inoperative as to the creature. For the life's will broke itself off therefrom, and went into sensibility, out of unity into plurality; it

strove against the Unity, viz. the eternal one rest, the one good.

7. When this took place, the divine ground (viz. the second Principle or the wisdom of God, which in divine power with the out-breathing will of God had imprinted itself in the image-like life [of the soul or of the first, fiery principle], as in the counterstroke to God) was eclipsed in the false will. For the cause of the motion of the holy Essence had turned itself to earthliness, in which evil and good are in strife.

8. Understand it: The eternal, unfathomable will of life had turned itself away from the divine Ens, and wished to rule in evil and good. And therefore the second principle, or the kingdom of God, is become extinguished for it; and in the stead thereof is arisen the third Principle in its own figurative form, as the quality of the stars and of the four elements; whence the body became coarse and animal, and the senses false and earthly.

9. Life has thus lost the temperament, viz. the eternal rest, and has by its own desire made itself dark, painful, harsh, hard and rough. It has become a mere restlessness, and runs now in earthly power in an eternal ground, and seeks rest in that which is frail or fragile, but finds none; for fragility is not life's equality. Therefore the life sets itself forcibly above the existence of this world, and dominates the mortal power of the stars and elements as an individual God of Nature. And it is by such domination become silly and foolish, so that in such earthly imagination (*Bildung*) and

self-assumption it cannot recognize its ground and original state, wherein its eternal rest stood; and is rightly called foolish. For it has brought itself out of the divine Ens into an earthly (animal) ens, and placed itself in a fragile being; and will rule in that which nevertheless perishes for it, and passes away quickly like a smoke.

10. And when that breaks, over which it has ruled for a while, then the life remains in its contrariety in the first principle, in darkness; and is nothing else than an everlasting, unquenchable, painful fire-source, as the devils also are such.

11. To the aid of this captive life came again the great love of God; and immediately after such downfall inbreathed itself again into the inward ens, viz. into the deadened nature of divine quality; and gave itself to the life for an object, introduced itself as a new fountain of divine unity, love and rest into the faded divine Ens, and revealed itself therein; from which the life is able to draw and its pain and restlessness in the *centra* of ownness to extinguish.

12. Further, this new fountain of divine love and unity has, by its outflow in Christ, embodied itself in the true life of all the three principles of human quality; and has entered into the image-like senses, viz. into life's natural, creaturely, dissentient, image-like will, and assumed humanity; and has shattered egoism and self-will by the influence of the one love of God, as by the eternal One; and turned life's will inwards again to the eternal One, to the temperament, whereby the devil's introduced will was destroyed, and

life's painfulness brought into the true rest.   And has broken open the shutting-in, viz. death, and restored again the divine paradisaic budding with the holy senses and workings; and led the holy life through the confining of death, and made death and the devil's will a reproach.   And has thus powerfully demonstrated how the eternal One can predominate over plurality and particularity, that the might of what is image-like may not be a God, but the might of what is super- and un-image-like rule all.   For what is image-like is only a counterstroke to the un-image-like will of God, through which the will of God works.

13. But seeing the great love of God in Christ is thus come to the aid of human life in earthly form, and has made for us poor men in the life of the humanity of Christ an open gate of grace to the divine entrance;   therefore the matter now lies in this, that the life's will taken captive in its image-like existence should abandon again the earthly, viz. egoism and self-will, and immerse itself wholly and solely in this embodied grace (which pressed from one, as from the first man, upon all, Rom. v. 18);   and take to itself this grace, and in virtue of such acceptance and divine union sink with the resigned life's will into the super-sensible, superfathomable, eternal One, as into the first ground of life's beginning, and give itself up again to the ground from which life sprang forth; then it is again in its eternal place, in the temperament, in the true rest.

14. Reason says: How can a man do this, seeing the Scripture saith (1 Cor. xv. 45; Gen. i. 28):

The first man was made a natural life, to rule over all the creatures and beings of this world. The life must therefore introduce desire into earthly quality. Answer. Human life is placed in a counterstroke to the divine will, in and through which counterstroke God wills; and the earthly creatures are placed in a counterstroke to human life, in and through which counterstroke man was to will. Man's will was with God's will to will, and rule over all natural and creaturely life. Not in animal but in divine essence was it to stand. Though man was placed with life in Nature, yet his nature was a temperament, and his life a mansion of divine will.

15. But because life must stand during this time in earthly essence, and cannot be rid of it, we must look at the threefold nature of the life according to the three principles; by which principle of the life man may plunge into the supersensible being of God, and how this may be done.

16. Christ said : Without me ye can do nothing (John xv. 5). No man can of his own power reach the supreme ground, unless he sink his inmost ground of the first principle, according to the life's image-like nature, in the embodied grace of God; and, in accordance with the same ground, stand still from his own being in divine hope, and give himself up wholly with the will to God, in such a way that his will no longer wills to speak according to this ground, save what God speaks and wills through this ground; then he is at the highest goal.

17. If it be possible for him to stand still an hour

or less from his own inner willing and speaking, then will the divine will speak into him. By which inspeaking God's will embraces his will in Himself, and speaks into the image-like, natural, external Reason-life; and dissolves and illuminates the earthly imagination of Reason's will, so that immediately the supersensible divine life and will buds and incentres itself in Reason's will.

18. For as little as the life's own will can, in selfness and will turned away from God, stand still in Nature a moment from its working, unless it sink down beyond all Nature; so little also can the divine speaking, in the life resigned to the ground, stand still from its working.

19. For if the life stand still from its own will, it is in the abyss of Nature and creation, in the eternal, divine utterance; and hence God speaks therein.

20. For from God's speaking the life has proceeded and come into body, and is nothing else than an image-like will of God. Now if its own imagination and will stand still, the divine imagination and will arises. For whatever is will-less is with the Nothing but one thing, and is out of or beyond all Nature, which ungroundedness is God himself.

21. Seeing then the Unground or God is an eternal speaking, viz. a breathing forth of himself, the Unground accordingly is inspoken into the resigned life; for the breathing of the Unground speaks through the stationary ground of the life. For the life has arisen from the divine breathing, and is a likeness of the divine breathing, therefore

one likeness seizes the other. As we understand
in the case of the life's senses, which are such an
issue from the breathing of the soul, as the soul
is an issue and counterstroke from the divine soul
of the divine knowledge.

22. Now as God, by his breathing forth of his
eternal wisdom and knowledge, has revealed himself by Nature and creation, both by the inward
holy life, by the life of angels and men, and has
introduced his will of his knowledge into form
for re-utterance through a formed divulged mode ;
as also by Nature and its re-breathing forth of the
creatures of the visible world, and has always
made the external, uttered by Nature, subject to
the inward principle, so that the inward should
rule through the external corporeal, and be a spirit
of the external :

23. Know, then, that in like manner, the intro-
verted, new-born life of man, in divine power
and might, can and should rule over the external
Reason-life of stars and elements. And if this be
not done—viz. that the inward eternal life in man,
in divine power and light, rule over the external,
earthly, astral life of the mortal desire, and break
the will of the earthly desire (wherein lies the
serpent's image)—then there is not yet any new
birth or divine will manifest in such life and working, and such a man (as long as he stands in the
earthly will alone) is no child of heaven. For the
divine scientia is transformed into earthly, animal
quality by the individual imagination of the false
will ; and is as to the body an evil beast, and as
to the soul an averse, false will, which wills not

with God—after the manner of the devils, who likewise stand in their own imagination of sensual knowledge.

24. Therefore Christ said (Matt. xii. 30) : He that gathereth not with me scattereth. That is, whosoever works, wills and acts not with the embodied divine grace, which God through Christ has revealed and offers, but works by natural individual will, he disperses not only the divine order of the senses, but scatters also his works into false ground.

25. Consider a parable of the sun. If a herb hath not sap, the sun's rays scorch it; but if it hath sap, the sun's rays warm it, whereby it grows. So also in the life of essence in man. Hath that life not ens from God's gentleness and love, viz. from the eternal One, then it impresseth itself into a fierce, fiery sharpness, so that the mind becomes wholly rough, hungry, covetous, envious and stinging. And such false sense and will proceeds then from the life into the body, and into all its ways and works.

26. Such a fiery, covetous, envious nature with the life's sharp sense scatters and destroys all that is good. There is danger in all it has to do with. For it carries its poisonous rays thereinto, and will draw all to itself, and bring its poison thereinto, viz. hungry covetousness. But if it be that the fiery life can eat of divine love, then it is a similitude how a light presses forth from fire : Thus the right life presses forth from the fiery nature with a new spirit and will of divine love from within ; and is no longer taking, as the fire's

nature is, but giving. For the will of love gives itself, as light from fire, which gives itself to all things, and produces in all something that is good.

27. If the sun did shine no more in the deep of the world, then would the *spiritus mundi* in the sharpness of the stars, in the sulphureous, mercurial nature in the four elements, be wholly stern, rough, dry, harsh, thick, dark, and hard. Hence all life in the elements would perish, and it would soon be seen what hell and God's wrath are.

28. And thus in like manner as the outer man is a *limus* of the external elemental world, whose life has its subsistence in the power and virtue of the sun and stars, and the body, as also the earth, is a coagulation of the *spiritus mundi* ; and if that were unable to have in its food the sun's power of light and of love, it would become wholly evil, fiery, and mortal, and the external life would necessarily perish :

29. So also, in like manner, the soul is a *limus* of the inward spiritual world from the *Mysterium magnum,* viz. from the issue and counterstroke of the divine knowledge, which must receive its nourishment from the *Mysterium magnum* of the divine power and knowledge. Now if it cannot have the ens of divine love for its food, so that it breaks itself off from the unground, as from resignation or renunciation, then it becomes sharp, fiery, dark, rough, stinging, envious, hostile, rebellious, and an entire restlessness itself ; and introduces itself into a mortal, dying, fierce source, which is its damnation, wherein it goes to destruction, as befell the devil, and likewise befalls the wicked.

30. But if such a fire-source can again attain and receive in itself divine love, viz. the essential light of God, then this fire-source of the soul becomes transformed into a kingdom of joy, into praise to God. But without will that has turned round. that stands still from its own impression and shutting-in, this is not possible. For the light of the sun cannot so work in a hard stone as in herbs and trees, for the water is compacted and coagulated in the stone into a hard impression.

31. And thus it is to be understood with regard to the soul's false own will and divine gentleness, so that in such a covetous, envious fire-greed the divine gentleness accomplishes no working. Hence Christ truly said (John vi. 53): The life of man which should not eat the bread that is come from heaven to give life to the world, has no life in it. Thereby he indicates the essential love which God has manifested in him (in Christ) by a new fountain for refreshment of the poor withered soul. The soul that should not eat thereof cannot attain the divine Light, and were without divine life. And indeed he calls himself (John viii. 12) the Light of the world. Item, in the Psalms: A Light that shines in the darkness, which changes the darkness into light (Ps. cxii. 4).

CHAPTER III

Of the natural ground. How Nature is a counterstroke
to the divine knowledge, whereby the eternal (one)
will with the unfathomable, supernatural know-
ledge makes itself perceptible, visible, effectual,
and desireful. And what Mysterium magnum
is. How all is from, through, and in God. How
God is so near all things, and fills all.

A highly precious gate, for the reader that loveth
God to well consider.

John i. 1–3 runs thus : In the beginning was
the Word, and the Word was with God, and the
Word was God. The same was in the beginning
with God. All things were made by him, and
without him was not anything made that was made.

1. The beginning of all beings was the Word as
the breath of God ; and God was the eternal One
of eternity, and likewise remains so in eternity.
But the Word is the efflux of the divine will or
of the divine knowledge. As the senses flow from
the soul, and yet the soul is but a one ; so it was
with the eternal One in the efflux of the will, that
is to say : In the beginning was the Word. For
the Word as the efflux of the will of God is the
eternal beginning, and remains so eternally. For
it is the revelation of the eternal One, by and

through which the divine power is brought into a knowledge of somewhat. By the Word we understand the revealed will of God; and by the word God we mean the hidden God, viz. the eternal One from which the Word eternally springs forth.

2. Thus the Word is the efflux of the divine One, and yet God himself as his revelation.

3. This efflux flows from God; and what has flowed forth is wisdom, beginning and cause of all powers, colours, virtues and qualities.

4. From such a revelation of powers, in which the will of the eternal One contemplates itself, flows the understanding and the knowledge of the something (*Ichts*),[1] as the eternal will contemplates itself in the something (*Ichts*), and in wisdom introduces itself into delight in a likeness and image.

5. This image is the *Mysterium magnum*, viz. the creator of all beings and creatures; for it is the separator in the efflux of the will, which makes the will of the eternal One separable; it is the separability in the will, from which powers and qualities arise.

6. These powers again are an efflux of themselves, each power bringing itself into individual will according to the virtue of that same power. From thence arises the multiplicity of wills, and from this also the creaturely life of eternity has taken its origin, viz. angels and souls. And yet it cannot be said that by this a Nature or creation is understood, but the eternal imaged existence of the

---

[1] *Ichts* the opposite of *Nichts* (nothing) is "I," self-consciousness. — Hegel, *Hist. of Phil.*, vol. iii. p. 286.

divine word and will, as the Spirit of God has in such a counterstroke, in the powers of wisdom, sported with himself in such formation of similitude.

7. As the mind of man in the understanding introduces itself by the senses into a counterstroke of an exact likeness, and by sense flows forth and disposes into images, which images are the thoughts of the mind, wherein the will of the mind works, and thus by desire brings itself into a sharpness, as into a magnetic appropriation, from which joy and sorrow arise;

8. So also, in regard to the eternal mind of perceptibility, we are to understand that the outgoing of the one will of God has, through the Word, introduced itself into separability, and the separability has introduced itself into receptibility, as into desire and craving for its self-revelation, passing out of the Unity into plurality.

9. Desire is the ground and beginning of the nature of perceptibility of the particular will. For therein is the separability of the Unity brought into receptibility, whence the separabilities of the wills are brought into perceptibility of a selfhood, wherein the true, creaturely, perceptible, angelic, and soulic life is understood.

10. For the will of the eternal One is imperceptible, without tendency to anything; for it has nothing to which it could tend, save only towards itself. Therefore it brings itself out of itself, and carries the efflux of its unity into plurality, and into assumption of selfhood, as of a place of a Nature, from which qualities take their rise.

For every quality has its own separator and maker within it, and is in itself entire, according to the quality of the eternal Unity.

11. Thus the separator of each will develops in its turn qualities from itself, from which the infinite plurality arises, and through which the eternal One makes itself perceptible, not according to the unity, but according to the efflux of the unity. But the efflux is carried to the greatest sharpness with magnetic receptivity, to the nature of fire; in which fiery nature the eternal One becomes majestic and a light. Thereby [by fire] the eternal power becomes desireful and effectual, and [fire] is the original condition of the sensitive life, where in the Word of power, in the efflux, an eternal sensitive life has its origin. For if life had no sensitiveness, it would have no will nor efficacy; but pain makes it effectual and capable of will. And the light of such kindling through fire makes it joyous, for it is an anointment of painfulness.

12. From this eternal operation of the sensation and sense-element, which very working has from eternity introduced itself into Nature and qualities, the visible world with all its host sprang, and was brought into a creaturely being. For the eternity of such working to fire, light and darkness has with visible world carried itself into a counterstroke, and made the separator in all the powers of the emanated being a steward of Nature, by whom the eternal will rules, makes, forms and shapes all things.

13. We can, therefore, in no wise say that God's

essence is something far off, which possesses a
special abode or place; for the abyss of Nature
and creation is God himself.

14. The visible world with its host of creatures
is nothing else than the emanated Word which
has disposed itself into qualities, as in qualities the
particular will has arisen. And with the receptibility of the Will the creaturely life arose; which
life has in the beginning of this world introduced
itself into a receptivity for a creaturely ground,
which the separator has separated according to
the quality, and brought to a will of its own after
such a fashion. And with the self-will of such
desire substance or body of its likeness and quality
has arisen to each receptivity; whereby the separator has signed itself and made itself visible, as
is to be seen in every life.

15. In this counterstroke of the divine will
we are to understand two kinds of life, viz. an
eternal and a temporal. That which is eternal
is in the Eternal, and arises from the eternal
Word. It stands at the basis of the eternal
spiritual world, in the *Mysterium magnum* of the
divine counterstroke, and constitutes the intel-
lective life at the basis of the eternal fire and
light.

16. The inmost ground is a spark of the emanated will of God through the eternal divine breathing, and is united with God's Word to will nothing
but what the one will of God wills through such
emanation.

17. It is nothing else than a mansion of divine
will, through which the divine will reveals itself;

and is revealed to no peculiarity of individual will, but only to the instrument of the divine will, by which this chooses to perform its marvellous works. It is the separator of the divine will, an instrument of God, into which the divine will has fashioned itself so as to be a wonder-worker of omnipotence and glory, by which he will rule all things. Wherefore also the divine understanding was given to it.

18. The other life is a primal efflux of the separator of all powers, and is called the soul of the outer world. This life became creaturely in the emanated qualities, and is a life of all the creatures of the visible world, whereby the separator or creator of this world fashions itself and makes a likeness of the spiritual world, in which the power of the inward spiritual world forms, shapes and beholds itself.

19. For the spiritual world of fire, light and darkness is hidden in the visible elemental world, and works through the visible world, and by the separator imprints itself with its efflux in all things, according to each thing's kind and quality. According as each several thing is of a kind and quality, such a quality does it receive from the separator of the inward spiritual power. Not for a possession and individual power does the visible receive the invisible, that the outer might thereby be transformed into the inner. No; that is not so. The inward power fashions itself in the way we understand this in the powers of herbs, trees and metals, that their external spirit is only an instrument of the inward spirit or of the inward power,

whereby the inward power imprints itself in the external spirit.

20. We understand indeed in such powers of growing things three kinds of *spiritus* in different *centra*, but in one *corpus*. The first and external *spiritus* is the coarse sulphur, salt and mercury, which is a substance of four elements, or of the stars according to the property of their roughness. It makes the *corpus*, and impresses itself or compacts itself into a substance, or draws that which is internal out of the spiritual separator into itself, as also the elements from without, and coagulates itself therewith; whence immediately the signature or sign is effected by the separator. It forms the visible *corpus* according to the property of the greatest power of the *spiritus mundi*, viz. according to the constellation of the stars or property of the planets and now enkindled elements.

21. The second *spiritus*, which has a *centrum* of its own, is found in the oil of sulphur, which is called the fifth essence, viz. a root of the four elements. This *spiritus* is the softening and joy of the coarse, painful spirit of sulphur and salt; and receives its nourishment, firstly, from within, from the light of Nature, from the efflux of spiritual gentleness, from the inward spiritual fire and light. And, secondly, it receives its nourishment from without, from the sun and from the subtle power of the *spiritus mundi*, and is the true cause of growing life, a joy of Nature, as is the sun in the elements.

22. The third *spiritus* is the tincture, a counter-

stroke of the divine *Mysterium magnum,* in which all powers are in equality, and is rightly called paradise or divine delight. It is a mansion of divine power, a mansion of the eternal soul, whence all external powers spring, after the manner of air from fire.

23. For the tincture is nothing else than a spiritual fire and light, in which fire and light is a single and united being. But because it has within it its separator, as the emanated divine will to manifestation, it is the highest reason for which the first separation of qualities comes about in the existence of this world, and belongs by its own quality to eternity. For its origin is the holy power of God. And it has a special *centrum,* viz. the most inward ground of the creature, which indeed is hidden to the mortal creature on this account, that man brought false will against it. Hence arose the curse of the earth at the fall of man. Yet this high, holy principle in its own *centrum* presses forth through all the beings of this world, and flows forth into the outer powers, as the sun into the elements. But the creature cannot touch the *centrum* of this power, unless it be done by divine permission, as comes to pass in the new birth.

24. Such a revelation is seen in all living and growing things. All things have their subsistence in these three principles or beginnings. You see an example in a herb of the earth, which has its nourishment from within and without, viz. from the earth, and from without from the sun and stars, whereby the *spiritus* of the earth together

with the external *spiritus* fashions itself. When the herb sprouts forth, it is in such power that this is realized. Thus the outward separator in sulphur, salt and mercury signs itself externally with the shape and form of the herb; for it is the herb's motion and sensation, and makes itself corporeal.

25. So that when I see a herb standing, I may say with truth: This is an image of the Earth-spirit, in which the upper powers rejoice, and regard it as their child; for the Earth-spirit is but one being with the upper, outward powers. And when the herb is grown up, it blossoms; and with the blossom the oleous spirit signs itself with beautiful colours. And with the lovely smell of the blossom, the tincture or the third principle signs itself.

26. Here then we understand that the inward, hidden spirit of the elements has revealed itself, and brings itself also into the form of the fruit. For the earth would have no such smell, neither colours nor such virtue, if the hidden power of the divine efflux did not manifest itself.

27. So also with metals, which outwardly are a coarse *corpus* of sulphur, mercury and salt, wherein consists the growth; but in their inward ground they are a beautiful clear *corpus*, in which the ideal light of Nature shines from the divine efflux. In this lustre is to be understood the tincture and great power, how the hidden power makes itself visible. It cannot be said of such power or virtue that it is elemental, as neither is the power of the blossom so. The elements are

only a mansion and counterstroke of the inward power, a cause of the motion of the tincture.

28. For power proceeds from the tincture through motion of the coarse elemental spirit, and is carried thereby into sensation, viz. into taste and smell.

29. For smell is nothing but the sensation of the tincture, through which the efflux of divine power reveals itself, and thus assumes perceptibility. The sharpness of smell is indeed elemental, but the true power and virtue in the sharpness of the smell is the tincture. For the motion of a thing is not the highest reason of power, but that to which the cause of the motion is due.

30. The physician uses a fragrant herb for his medicaments; but the smell, that is, the sharpness of the smell, is not the cure which cureth the patient in his sickness. But that is the cure, from which such balsam or smell arises, viz. the tincture, which imprints itself in such balsam.

31. Christ said to the fig-tree : Be thou withered (Matt. xxi. 19). But the external, audible, human word, or the sound, was not the power by which it was done. But the power was that from whence the word came. Else, if the external human sound did it, other men could do it too.

32. The like also is to be understood concerning faith. Confession and assent in respect to a thing is not true faith, much less is science so. But that is faith, from which the confession proceeds, viz. the revealed Spirit of God in the inward ground of the soul, which by the confession frames itself in the pronounced word and makes this visible

outwardly, and works with the visible elements of faith and exhibits itself outwardly. So that we understand that God's Spirit co-operates in the work of faith, just as it works with and through the power of the elemental world, and makes itself visible through the existence of this world with a counterstroke.

33. So that, as regards everything I look upon, be it evil or good, I can with truth say : Here, by this thing, has the hidden spirit of the separator of all beings shaped itself into a property, and made for itself here an object or image according to its efflux, either according to evil or good ; all according to the properties of Nature, according to heat or cold, according to harsh, bitter, sweet or sour, or however that may be. And in all such formation there is only outwardly such an elemental nature, viz. such a sulphur and salt ; but in the inward ground, in the tincture, it is good and profitable, and belongs to its likeness for the nourishment of life, which by the astral and elemental nature stands in all properties according to its external ground.

34. Every particular thing, be it herb, grass, tree, beast, bird, fish, worm, or whatsoever it be, is of use, and has proceeded from the separator of all beings, viz. from the Word or separable will of God, by which the separator of each thing's quality has made for itself a likeness or image in which it works.

35. For this visible world with all its host and being is nothing but an objective representation of the spiritual world, which spiritual world is

hidden in this material, elemental world, like as the tincture in herbs and metals.

36. And as the tincture with its virtue fashioneth itself in all things with its efflux and makes itself visible, so that we may see and know by the figure, as well as by the colours and smell, what manner of separator or efflux of divine will has emanated in the tincture from the *Mysterium magnum*; so likewise we may recognize in the visible world, in sun, stars, elements and all creatures, the inward ground from which they arose.

37. For no thing or being is come from afar to its place, but in the place where it grows is its ground. The elements have their cause, from which they arise, in themselves; the stars also have their chaos, wherein they stand, in themselves.

38. The elements are nothing but an image-like, moving existence of what is invisible and non-moving.

39. The stars likewise are an efflux of the qualities of the spiritual world, according to the separation of the separator, whose ground is the Word or the separable will of God.

40. The being and motion of the elements is fire, air, water and earth, wherein is thick and thin, moist and dry, hard and soft, and these are united together in one substance. Not that each is from a particular origin, but they all proceed from a single ground, and that place where they have arisen is everywhere. We have only to conceive how at one place there may have been a greater enkindling according to one quality than at another place,

whereby the motion has become greater, and of material things in such form and substance more have been produced than at another place. As is to be understood by the material things of the earth, as also by the water and air, how a difference exists at each pole, or at each position above the earth. Whence also the difference of manners and of virtues, as well as of governments, laws and creatures.

41. But the differences of such qualities have all arisen from the *Mysterium magnum*, by the motion once for all of the powers of all beings, as when the one will of all beings put itself in motion at once, and brought itself out of non-perceptibility into perceptibility and separability of powers, and made the eternal Power effectual and desireful, so that in each power a counterstroke as an individual desire has arisen. This same desire in the counterstroke of the powers has developed itself in its turn out of itself into a counterstroke, whence the desire of such efflux is become acute, strong and excessive, and has coagulated and brought itself into material things.

42. And as the efflux of the inward powers has been from light and darkness, from sharpness and gentleness, from the nature of fire or of light, so has been the origination of material things. The further the efflux of a power has extended, the more outward and coarse does the matter become; for one counterstroke has proceeded out of another, unto finally the coarse earth.

43. But we must deduce correctly the ground of this philosophy, and indicate whence hard

and soft have taken their origin.   This we recognize
in metals.   For every matter which is hard, as are
metals and stones, as also wood, herbs and the like,
has within it a very noble tincture and high spirit
of power.   As also is to be recognized in the bones
of creatures, how the noblest tincture according
to the power of the Light, or the greatest sweetness,
is in the marrow of the bones ; and, on the other
hand, in the blood there is only a fiery tincture,
viz. in sulphur, salt and mercury.   This is understood thus :

44. God is the eternal One, or the greatest
gentleness [stillness], so far as he exists in himself
independently of his motion and manifestation.
But in his motion he is called a God in trinity,
that is, a triune Being, where we speak of three
and yet but of one, and in accordance with which
he is called the eternal Power and Word.   This is
the precious and supreme ground, and thus to be
considered : The divine will shuts itself in a place
to selfhood, as to power, and becomes active in
itself ; but also by its activity goes forth, and
makes for itself an object, viz. wisdom, through
which the ground and origin of all beings has
arisen.

45. In like manner know this : All that is soft,
gentle and thin in the existence of this world is
emanating and self-giving ; and its ground and
origin is in accordance with the Unity of eternity,
the Unity perpetually emanating from itself.   And
indeed in the very nature of thinness or rarity,
as in water and air, we understand no sensation
or pain, so far as that nature is one in itself.

46. But whatever is hard and impressing, as bones, wood, herbs, metals, fire, earth, stones, and the like material things,—therein is the image of divine power and motion, and shuts itself up with its separator (viz. the efflux of divine desire) against the coarseness, as a noble jewel or sparkle of divine power. And it is hard and fiery on this account, that it hath its own ground of divine inclusion, as where the eternal One introduces itself continually into a ground of threefoldness for motion of powers, and yet shuts itself up against the efflux, as against the introduction of the particular will of Nature, and with the power of the Unity works through Nature.

47. And so it is to be understood in regard to the noble tincture. Where it is noblest, there it is most of all shut up with the hardness. For the Unity is involved in it in a mobility, as in a sensation of activity, and therefore it is hidden ; but in thinness or rarity it is involved not in such sensation, but is one with all things. As indeed water and air are one with all things, and are in all things. But the dry water is the true pearly foundation, in which the subtle power of the working of the Unity is in the centre. To ours, who are worthy of this, it is hereby intimated, that they should not give their attention to the soft and yielding apart from the fiery nature, to seek the mystery therein. Understand this mystery thus :

48. That the soft and thin arises from the Unity, from its emanation, from the *Mysterium magnum*, and is nearest to the Unity ; and, on the other

hand, the noblest ground of divine revelation, both in power and operation, lies in the fiery hardness, and is a dry unity or a temperament, wherein again is contained the separability of all powers. For, where powers are comprised not in the unity of a will, there the will is divided, and no great power is to be understood in that thing. Which ought well to be observed by the physicians, that they should not look to the coarse *spiritus* of strong smell, and regard that as the true balsam; although it is present therein, and so is the tincture therein very mobile and evolant.

49. The *spiritus* or spiritual essences of the strong power in smell must be brought into the temperament, into unity, and not be flying from it, whereby men attempt to cure with salt, as with the sharpness of fire, and give to the patient soul without spirit.

50. The soul of such balsams is separated in the qualities; each one gives itself in its great joy separately, but in separation they are too rebellious. They unite not life's enmity and division, but kindle life's division more.

51. Shut them up and make them one, so that they all have one will in love, and you have the pearl of the whole world. To provoke to wrath causes pride and strife, which is to be recognized in all things.

52. A prisoner is comforted only by his release, until he place his will in hope, and compose himself with patience; and so at last his restlessness falls into hope, into the temperament, and he learns

in such hope to become humble. Then, if one tells him of his release, he rejoices.

53. Therefore, ye physicians, observe it, that is your pearl, if you can understand this, the meaning is internal and external.

CHAPTER IV

Of the In and Out. How the eternal will of God carries itself outwards and into perceptibility, inwards and again into the One.

Here may be understood to what end the being of this world was created, and what purpose the creaturely ground serves. Further, to what end joy and sorrow have become manifest; and how God is so near all things.

1. John i. 11–13 runs thus : He (Jesus Christ) came unto his own, and his own received him not. But as many as received him, to them gave he power to become children of God, even to them that believe on his name : which were born, not of blood, nor of the will of the flesh, nor of the will of man, but of God.

2. In these words we have the precious ground of divine revelation, viz. the eternal In and Out. For they speak of this, how the hidden divine eternal Word of the divine power of the Unity came forth into the emanated, natural, creaturely, image-like Word, viz. into humanity, into his own.

3. For the emanated, image-like, creaturely Word is the ever-speaking Word's property. And it is thereby clearly signified that his own, or the averse, image-like, particular will, received him

not. This individual, image-like will had arisen from its own ground, viz. from flesh and blood of the self-ful nature of man and woman, that is, in the separator of the emanated will, where the eternal will had confined itself in ownership, and would go forth and rule in personal power and might.

4. This received not the eternal Word (which, as an outflow of divine grace, again came forth to the averse will), for it would be an individual lord. But the will which has turned round, so that it has been born anew in the divine outflow of love, to that gave he power to become God's child. For it is not the natural, individual will can inherit the divine childship, but only that which, united with the Unity, is one with all things, in which God himself works and wills.

5. Wherein we clearly understand how the inward ground has extroverted itself and made itself visible, and is a peculiar possession of God, as an efflux of divine power and will.

Selected Ann Arbor Paperbacks
Works of enduring merit

For a complete list of Ann Arbor Paperback titles write:
THE UNIVERSITY OF MICHIGAN PRESS ANN ARBOR